West Norfolk Fertilisers 1872-1965

The story of one of the former, major industrial concerns in King's Lynn, known locally as the "muck works", with memories by former employees.

W.F. Sampson,
Clenchwarton,
King's Lynn.

September, 1993.

ACKNOWLEDGEMENTS

The author would like to say thank you, to the many people who have loaned photographs and given their memories, also to

Mr Bob Pinnock, for his valuable help,

Mrs Phyllis Carter, for her patience in editing this work,

Mr Alan Mews and True's Yard for their help in typesetting,

the staff of the Norfolk Record Office, the Lynn Museum and the Lynn Library, the Editor of the Lynn News and Mr R Goodchild for their help and assistance and, finally,

my wife, Joyce, for her wholehearted support.

W.F. Sampson. 1993.

Printed by Colour Print of Fakenham.

copyright © W.F. Sampson 1993.
All rights reserved. No part of this publication may be reproduced, stored in a retrieval system, or transmitted in any form or by any means, electronic, mechanical, photocopying, recording or otherwise, without the prior permission of the author.

ISBN 0 9522132 0 6

CONTENTS

Chapter 1	OVERTURE	5
Chapter 2	THE FIRST EMPLOYEES	9
Chapter 3	THE GROWTH OF THE COMPANY	16
Chapter 4	THE TAR WORKS	34
Chapter 5	WORK ON THE FLOORS	39
Chapter 6	WOMEN IN THE WORKS	51
Chapter 7	THE DENS	54
Chapter 8	THE ACID PLANTS	59
Chapter 9	SUPPLIES AND DISPATCH	69
Chapter 10	THE OFFICE STAFF	77
Chapter 11	THE ENGINEERS	83
Chapter 12	THE LABORATORY	90
Chapter 13	BOAL QUAY	94
Chapter 14	BOSTON WORKS	96
Chapter 15	NITROGEN FERTILISERS	98
Chapter 16	SPRAYING ON THE FARMS	100
Chapter 17	A PASSION FOR SPORTS	102
Chapter 18	SAFETY	106
Chapter 19	THE 1940's-1960's EXPANSION PROGRAMME	114
Chapter 20	FINALE	131
Index		133

LIST OF ILLUSTRATIONS

Page one of the first Minute Book 7
The Company's first advertisement 8
Employees in front of new work's power station, c.1900-1910 15
'Adulteration' advertisement 17
The old works, 1910 20
Thomas Brown 22
James Brown 23
Dr. H.C. Brown 25
Work's A.R.P. personnel 27
Work's A.R.P. personnel (fire section) 28
E.H.I. Brown 30
Retirement ceremony 32
Royal Norfolk Show, Anmer, June 1950 33
Royal visit to the showstand, June 1950 33
Battery of stills, 1910, showing part of pitch lake or beck 35
The tar works, 1910, showing stills 36
Page of an employee's notebook, 1915-1923 40
Interior of one of the sheds, 1932 48
A break from one of the floors, c. 1932 49
Three working ladies, c. 1918 51
Alice Rockett with a group of workers, c. 1932 53
The Moritz lead chamber acid plant, 1951 67
The yard at the old works, 1933 70
The pyrites truck tippler 72
Les Figgis at the controls of 'Patricia.' 73
Building a stack 74
One of the loading stages at River shed, 1933 76
Mary Hampson 78
The main workshop, c. 1950 84
The main laboratory, c. 1950 92
The 'Sea Venture' at Boal Quay, 1933 95
The Foden steam lorry in a ditch 97
Filling the sprayer with water before adding the acid, c. 1933 100
Offloading sprayer from Foden steam lorry 101
The domino team, c. 1950 104
The bowls team 104
The cricket section, c. 1954 105
The new first aid treatment room, 1962 109
Safety exhibition in work's hall, 1962 110
Jack Roberts 113
The old granulation plant, c. 1950 115
The process building foundations taking shape 118
Nar shed 119
The granulation plant in operation 120
New shed showing heaps of superphosphate 121
The aftermath of the flood at the old works granulation plant 123
The ball mill 125
The pilot plant, c. 1950 127
Aerial view of the site, c. 1953 130

Chapter 1

OVERTURE

On Tuesday 6th August, 1872, four Norfolk farmers and a chemist held the first board meeting of the West Norfolk Farmers' Manure Company Limited, in temporary offices at 63, High Street, King's Lynn. (The Midland Bank stands there today).

Thomas Brown was appointed managing director and acting secretary, at an annual salary of £150. In addition he received four free shares in the Company.

Thirty four years old, Thomas Brown was born at Middleton, Suffolk, the eldest son of John Brown, a local builder. One of five brothers, Thomas was educated at Yoxford Academy, Kesgrave School and Highbury College. He became a schoolteacher and taught at a school in Holbrook, Suffolk. In 1862 he was appointed by the Bishop of Norwich as headmaster of an endowed grammar school at Grimston, Norfolk, teaching both boarders and day boys.

It was at Grimston that Thomas Brown started to apply his extensive knowledge of chemistry and love of agriculture. Beginning as an agricultural merchant, he started to make and test manures such as superphosphate of lime; to accomplish this he bought coprolite and sulphuric acid. (A joke in the family was that he used to make superphosphate in a 'copper'). He also imported nitrate of soda and guano into Lynn.

Thomas was writing in Norwich papers on agricultural matters and also conducting experiments. In 1870, in conjunction with a Dr Augustus Voelcker, he carried out trials with the use of potash on the mangold crop and imported into Lynn 200 tons of 'kainit' from Germany. It is believed that this was the first shipment of this source of potash into Great Britain. The results of a set of these experiments were described in the Journal of the Royal Agricultural Society in 1871 by Dr Voelcker.

As a result of being boycotted by certain manufacturers, he found it increasingly difficult to purchase the acid needed to produce superphosphate, so he resigned his scholastic appointment at the grammar school and with a group of Norfolk farmers decided to form the "West Norfolk Farmers' Manure Company."

Up to 30th June, 1873, 31 shares of £500 each had been 'taken up' by eleven people.

The Founder Members of the Company		
1. Horace Beck	Harpley	Farmer
2. George Brereton	Flitcham	Farmer
3. Thomas Brown	King's Lynn	Chemist
4. William Betts	Flitcham	Farmer
5. Alfred Oldfield	Grimston	Farmer
6. Herbert E Ringer	Rougham	Farmer
7. John Wellingham	Walton	Farmer
8. Horace Lock Ringer	Rougham	Farmer
9. John B Ellis	West Barsham	Farmer
10. Charles Betts	Ashill	Farmer
11. William Blomfield	Necton	Farmer

courtesy of Norfolk Record Office

In 1872, a site of approximately seven and a half acres was rented at £23 per year from a Mr J.M. Bird. The site was fronted at the north end by the Wisbech Road and bordered along the east side by the River Nar. It consisted mainly of marshy land which was frequently flooded at Spring tides, so it had to be drained and a sea bank raised, before a factory could be built, which included an acid plant, a mill and a tar works. The builder was a Mr Edgar Hall.

After three months, Thomas Brown was joined by his 25 year old brother James, who had also been a teacher and had worked in the USA and in Newcastle-upon-Tyne. He became the accountant.

At a Meeting of the Members of "The West Norfolk Farmers' Manure Company" Limited held at the Temporary Offices of the Company in High Street, Lynn on Tuesday the 6th day of August 1872.

Present – Messrs. H. Beck, C. Brereton, W. Betts, F. Ringer & J. Brown.

It was moved by Mr. Brereton & seconded by Mr. Betts and resolved unanimously that Mr. Beck be Chairman for the ensuing 12 months.

It was moved by Mr. Beck and seconded by Mr. Betts & resolved unanimously that all the Members who had subscribed the Memorandum of Association as registered be Directors of the Company namely the five Gentlemen present at this Meeting & Messrs. A. Oldfield & J. Willingham.

It was moved by Mr. Betts and seconded by Mr. Ringer and resolved unanimously that Mr. Brown be requested to act as Secretary of the Company until a regular Secretary is appointed to that Office.

Page one of the first Minute Book
courtesy of Norfolk Record Office

THE WEST NORFOLK
FARMERS' MANURE COMPANY,
LIMITED.

DIRECTORS.
Horace Beck, Harpley.
William Betts, Flitcham.
George Brereton, Flitcham.
Alfred Oldfield, Grimston.
Herbert Ringer, Rougham.
John Wellingham, Walton.

Managing Director, THOMAS BROWN, 63, High Street, Lynn.

THIS Company has been formed for the purpose of manufacturing MANURES, and obtaining, by means of Co-operation, the best feeding materials at lowest possible prices.

The Shareholders, consisting of farmers in West Norfolk, have resolved on this step in order to secure themselves from fraud or imposition. They will themselves require a considerable proportion of the manure which it will be possible to manufacture the first year, and already a large amount of the remainder has been contracted for. The Works are being erected as quickly as possible. As soon as the Factory is completed, the Superintendent will be instructed to allow any Norfolk Farmer to inspect the process adopted, and to examine or take samples of the materials employed, or of the manufactured articles.

Samples of the Manures will be periodically sent to Dr VOELCKER, and PROFESSOR SIBSON, and their suggestions carefully adopted, in order to secure the production of fertilizers of the very highest character.

The Company has now on hand, Wheat Manure, Rape and Cotton Cakes for the Wheat Crop.

Prices at the Lynn Railway Station, or at the Works.

WHEAT MANURE in bags, £7 per ton.
COTTON CAKES .... £5 10s ,,
BLACK SEA RAPE CAKES £5 15s ,,
GREEN RAPE CAKES .... £6 17s 6d ,,

Owing to the disturbed state of the labour market, it is impossible to quote a price for next Season's Manures. As soon as the contracts have been made for the delivery of the raw material, quotations will be made.

A cargo of Nitrate of Soda will arrive direct from Peru in January, or early in February next.

A cargo of American Bag Linseed Cake made from East India Seed is expected shortly from America. Others will follow.

It being the intention of the Company to treat directly with the consumer, its representative will regularly attend each of the principal markets in the district.

At present samples can be obtained and orders received at Stand 93, Corn Hall, Lynn, or at the Company's Offices, 63, High Street, Lynn.

The first advertisement, 5.10.1872
Courtesy of the Lynn News

Chapter 2

THE FIRST EMPLOYEES

The first record of employees appears in a wages book which begins with the week ending 18th September, 1874. This lists the names of nineteen men and a boy; unfortunately, no initials are given.

\multicolumn{5}{c|}{WNF Wages Book 18th September 1874}				
Name	Trade	Hours	Rate	Wages
Farrow	Carpenter	58.1/2	6d	£1. 9. 3
Hill	Millwright	58.1/2	6d	£1. 9. 3
Tinker	Miller	58.1/2	4.1/2d	£1. 1. 11
Tinker	Boy	58.1/2	1.1/4d	6. 1
Smith	Engine driver	58.1/2	5d	£1. 4. 4
Holdgate	Labourer	58.1/4	4d	19. 5
Curson	Labourer	43	4d	14. 4
Sharpin	Labourer	43	4d	14. 4
Medlock	Labourer	46.1/2	4.1/4d	16. 6
Goldsmith	Labourer	44.1/4	4d	14. 9
Hides	Labourer	58.1/2	4d	19. 6 1. 0
Caston	Labourer	58.1/2	4d	19. 6
Dye	Labourer	53.1/2	2.3/4d	12. 3
Shaftoe	Labourer	56	3.1/2d	16. 4
Davis	Tar distiller	78	5d	£1. 19. 0
Hiel	Tar distiller	76.1/2	4d	£1. 5. 6
Continued overleaf.				

9

Name	Trade		Wages
Fish	Fireman		£1. 3. 0
Groom	Fireman		£1. 3. 0
Hill	Timekeeper		5. 0
Medlock and Co - unloading			£2. 1. 4
Medlock and Co - loading			1. 5
Wagg - carting			£1. 2. 3

courtesy of Norfolk Record Office

Although most of the men were paid an hourly rate, a gang was operating on a piecework basis, unloading and loading materials.

By the week ending April 16th, 1875, the number of employees had increased to 27 men and a boy and the new names were Garne, Whitely, Dean, Avis, Johnson, Softley, Cassell, Skerry, Moore, Dans and two gentlemen called Smith. The total wages bill was £31.18. 8d and the hourly rate varied from 1.1/2d (boy's rate) to 7.1/4d (millwright).

Four additional employees are listed in the week ending September 17th, 1875. There is some evidence of expansion, mainly in the tar works, where the number of listed firemen has increased from two to four (Messrs Smith, Fysh, Groom and Whitely) and a 'presser' (Mr Moore), is recorded. There is also an additional carpenter (Mr Anger), a bricklayer (Mr Foreman), and a labourer (Mr Davis). The total wages bill was £24.14.2 for 31 men and a boy.

The next records available are for week ending April 12th, 1889, when initials were included.

WNF Wages Book April 12th, 1889			
Name	Trade	Hours	Rate	Wages
Savage I	Engineer	74.1/2	36/-pw	£2. 8. 0
Stinton T	Miller	56.1/2	26/-pw	£1. 6. 0
Continued overleaf.				

Stinton W	Engine driver	Full	22/6 pw	£1. 3. 2
Calton J	Labourer	63	4d	£1. 8. 3
Anger J	Carpenter	56.1/2	6.1/2d	£1. 10. 7
Hanwell H	Smith	74.1/2	30/-pw	£1. 19. 7
Arnold C	Smith's helper	-	12/-pw	15. 10
Guymer W	Labourer	63	4d	£1. 8. 3
Plowright T	Fireman	Full	24/-pw	£1. 13. 0
Fysh T	Fireman	Full	24/-pw	£1. 13. 0
Ashby A	Fireman	Full	28/-pw	£1. 8. 0
Smalley B	Fireman	Full	28/-pw	£1. 8. 0
Luckly J	Tar distiller	Full	30/-pw	£1. 15. 0
Evans G	Tar pressman	56.1/2	21/-pw	£1. 1. 0
Hancock W	Tar distiller	Full	27/-pw	£1. 11. 0
Curson J	Tar pressman	56.1/2	21/-pw	£1. 1. 0
Medlock W	Ganger	56.1/2	5.1/2d	£1. 6. 0
Plowright R	Mixer	59	4d	£1. 1. 8
Stinton B	Mixer	39.1/2	4d	13. 2
Ghem P	Mixer	39.1/2	4d	13. 2
Harvey R	Mixer	39.1/2	4d	13. 2
Barnes F.W	Labourer	52.1/2	4d	17. 6
Oakes E	Labourer	-	4d	10. 0
Paget G	Labourer	42.3/4	4d	14. 3
Farr J	Labourer	50.1/2	4d	16. 10
Day T	Labourer	Full	23/6pw	£1. 4. 6
Smith H	Labourer	56.1/2	4d	18. 10
Grainger A	Mill lad	56.1/2	10/-pw	10. 0
Continued overleaf.				

Name	Occupation			
Haverson J	Bagman	56.1/2	16/-pw	17. 0
Stinton S	Labourer	56.1/2	15/-pw	15. 0
Anger R	Carpenter	62.1/2	4d	£1. 10. 0
Appleton J	Cooper	57	24/-pw	£1. 4. 2
Smith J	Labourer	78	21/-pw	£1. 9. 0
Daisley E	Labourer	54.1/2	4d	18. 1
Oakes R	Horseman	52.1/2	4d	18. 6
Smith E	Labourer	56.1/2	15/6pw	£1. 2. 3
Overson J	Labourer	56.1/2	4d	18. 10
Waterson J	Engineer steam boat	Full	27/-pw	£1. 7. 0
Harrod F.W	Barge boy	Full	6/-pw	6. 0
Lee B	Bagman	Full	30/-pw	£1. 10. 0
Jackson B	Bagman	Full	21/-pw	£1. 1. 0
Dixon	Bagman	Full	21/-pw	£1. 1. 0
Fuller R	Labourer	30	4d	10. 0
Castle R	Labourer	56	4d	18. 8
Chapman F	Labourer	36.1/4	4d	12. 1
Mitchell	Labourer	56.1/2	4d	18. 10
Hiel T	Labourer	56.1/2	21/-pw	£1. 1. 0 5. 6
Shaul D	Labourer	56.1/2	14/-pw	14. 0
Burling W	Labourer	30.3/4	4d	10. 3
Oakes J	Labourer	36	4d	12. 0
Avis W	Labourer	56	4d	18. 8
Skerritt W	Labourer	55.1/2	4d	18. 6
Continued overleaf				

Catton E	Labourer	56.1/2	4d	18. 10
Morrison	Labourer	30.3/4	4d	10. 3
Goldsmith	Labourer	53.3/4	4d	17. 11
Pooley	Labourer	30.1/4	4d	10. 1
Mawby T	Labourer	30	4d	10. 0
Hewitt Chas	Labourer	30	4d	10. 0
Gayton W				£2. 12. 6
Robertson D				£2. 2. 6
Hill R.R				£1. 10. 0
Neal Geo				9. 0
Barnard A				4. 0
Medlock = Turtle - Breaking sulphur ore				£1. 1. 8
Lee B	Trip to Cambridge			£3. 18. 2
Burling H	Screening			£3. 14. 8
Avis H	Loading up. Unloading coal.			6. 1
Oakes H				£2. 1. 1
Eggett E	Carting			£3. 3. 0
Hewitt H	Screening			14. 2
Ghem H	Carrying out			£2. 0. 3
Nunn J	Labourer	31.1/2	4d	10. 6
Smith G	Knocking ammonia and harrowing sand			10. 0
Riches R	Carting			8. 0
				£84.19. 7

Courtesy of Norfolk Record Office

The first recorded list of salaried employees appears in a weekly salaries book beginning at the week ending November 29th 1902 and 17 members of staff are listed.

Weekly Salaries Book - Commencing Week Ending 29.11.1902			
Morgan F.W	(Weekly)	£3. 0. 0
Fenn H.J		£2. 0. 0
Kay J		£3. 0. 0
Brown J.S		£1. 10. 0
Taylor W		£1. 10. 0
Golden W		10. 0
Fryer A.J		10. 0
Trufett C (later C Truffit) Monthly 1/12 of £25		£2. 1. 8
Barron A.E		£1. 5. 0
Suggett		18. 0
Twite E		18. 0
Gamble F		7. 0
Brown H.H	(4 weeks)	£8. 0. 0
Athey J	(1 month)	£10. 0. 0
Hill R.R	(4 weeks)	£10. 0. 0
Targett B.M		£1. 5. 0
Leverington C		£2. 2. 0
New Names Added.		
Week ending:	Name:	
20.12.1902	Foreman F	
10.01.1903	Cutting Percival	
2.02.1903	Sheppard A	
2.04.1903	Hammond Wm	
4.02.1904	Broad E (began 17.02.1904 5/- per week)	
3.09.1905	Johnson James B (7/- per week)	
Continued overleaf.		

27.01.1906	Thurston W.L (£1.0.0. per week)
5.04.1906	Brown E
28.11.1906	Hardy John (5/- per week)
3.01.1907	Fitzgerald J (£1.10.0 per week) Brooks Leslie (began 21.01.1907, 7/-pw)
4.04.1907	Abel A.W (temporary clerk)
7.05.1908	Brown George (£2.10.0 per week)

Courtesy of Norfolk Record Office

Photograph taken in front of the New Works power station. Date unknown but estimated to be circa 1900-1910
courtesy of R Rout

Chapter 3

THE GROWTH OF THE COMPANY

The first eight years saw steady progress and increasing financial return. The table shows the dividend per share over that period; the cost of one share being £500.

Dividend Account Book		
Year ending	Dividend/Share	Income tax/Share
30.06.1873	£13. 19. 7	4/7d
30.06.1874	£50. 0. 0	-
30.06.1875	£100. 0. 0	12/-
30.06.1876	£50. 0. 0	12/6d
30.06.1877	£75. 0. 0	18/9d
30.06.1878	£100. 0. 0	£2. 1. 8d
30.06.1879	£100. 0. 0	£2. 1. 8d
30.06.1880	£125. 0. 0	Unknown

courtesy of Norfolk Record Office

Early Board Meetings and Annual General Meetings were held in the Globe Hotel, Lynn.

The primary aim of the directors was to produce quality fertilisers economically and to recipes that would suit individual soil conditions.

The Company was also testing other manufacturers' fertilisers and occasionally finding on examination that the contents did not always match the description; one fertiliser, described as containing dissolved bone, was found to be made from compounds and did not contain any bone at all.

Thomas Brown campaigned against this practice of debasing fertilisers with materials of substandard quality and was continually urging farmers to buy on unit values and thus avoid adulteration and inferior quality.

ADULTERATION
AND INFERIOR QUALITY IN
ARTIFICIAL MANURES

Can best be avoided by buying on UNIT VALUES.

THE WEST NORFOLK FARMERS' MANURE CO., LTD.,
KING'S LYNN,

Are prepared to supply their usual Stock Manures in Bags, free on rail, or to prepare any other Mixture to order, at

2/6 per unit for SOLUBLE PHOSPHATE.
10/- ,, ,, AMMONIA.
3/6 ,, ,, POTASH.

In Bone Manures only, the Phosphates not Soluble, are charged 2/- per Unit.

Dissolved Bones. Guaranteed 37 per cent. total Phosphate & 3 per cent. Ammonia.

Orders received at the Offices of the Company, or at Stand 99, Corn Exchange, Lynn

---

courtesy of the Lynn News

Thomas Brown gave a paper at the Norfolk Chamber of Agriculture on February 21, 1891, which supported a Bill for the 'better prevention of fraud in the manufacture and sale of artificial manures', etc. (This was Channing's Bill which was a forerunner of the 1893 Fertiliser and Feeding Stuffs Act)

The Company were also standard bearers for the interests of agriculture and were continually urging the government to offer a bonus or subsidy for growing wheat. They were among the first to publicise the growing of sugar beet in this country, having realised the potential by carrying out experiments on farms having varying soil conditions.

The continued prosperity led to a reward for employees in 1888 with a trip to Yarmouth for the men and their wives with a 'dinner and tea'; clerks and foremen were given gratuities. These trips to the seaside and annual small bonuses became regular events.

In order to fund further expansion, an offer was made by two of the directors in 1891, to lend the Company £1000 each at a low rate of interest. This was to pay for new plant for tar, ammonia and acid, new buildings and a barge.

In 1892, Dr Henry Charles Brown was officially appointed secretary of the Company and assistant manager. He was also allowed to accept the post of Borough Analyst for Lynn. A son of Thomas, the managing director, he was born near Ipswich and was educated at Owen's College, Manchester and in Germany and Switzerland.

In 1893 a new company was formed called the West Norfolk Farmers' Manure and Cattle Food Company Limited.

In the following year more cash was raised for further expansion by issuing mortgage debentures to directors and shareholders at £100 each paying 5% interest.

Mr Alfred Oldfield, a director, died in 1893 and directors and shareholders tendered for his shares. (WNF shares were never quoted on the stockmarket and were disposed of privately, mainly to existing shareholders or farmers wishing to become shareholders).

The new company lasted for a mere four years and was liquidated in 1897 (James Brown was the liquidator) and a new company was formed called the West Norfolk Farmers' Manure and Chemical Company Limited.

The following year debentures were issued at £1000 each to raise more money for expansion. (250 were issued between 5.8.1898 and 7.1. 1901).

In order to secure advances on their current account the directors deposited the title deed and writing relating to the Company's land and property in South Lynn with their bankers.

They continued to enlarge the works, building sheds for manure, enlarging the tar works and increasing warehouse space at the new works. They purchased a tug boat and had another barge constructed and they leased more land and had cottages built for foremen and workmen.

In 1908 they paid £450 for a motor car. (Three years later they had the body completely covered in.) In 1911 they purchased 100 gallons of petrol (called motor spirit in those days) at 1/2d per gallon. As they had no storage facilities, fifty-two gallon cans were bought to keep it in!

Stock taking was carried out annually. The one undertaken in 1910 was recorded in an invoice book and is interesting because of the wide range of materials held.

INVOICE BOOK No. 6 1910-1912
Stock taking carried out by B Ellis, T Brown and H.C Brown
June 20th, 1910

Coal tar stocks
Creosote, carbolic acid, cresylic acid, light oil, naphtha, green oil, green oil plus anthracene from stills, grease oil, pyridine, black varnish, creosote, salts, creosote salts pressed and ditto, drained and undrained, pitch, dusts, coals, anthracene. Casks.

Sulphuric acid 400 tons @ 30/- per ton = £600.0.0.

Phosphate stocks
Algerian high, ground and 68%, Tunisian high and low, Belgian, Coosaw, Florida rock, French, Gafsa, Norwegian. Bone ash, bone meal, bone trimmings, hoof and horn meal, Indian bone flour, Continental bone meal, bone flour, Liebeg, bone flour, Liebeg guano, dried blood, distillery waste, basic, slag, Peruvian guano, high and low.
Dissolved bone, supers 26%, 32%, 35%

Sulphate of potash magnesia,. muriate of potash, sulphate of potash, cyanamide (nitrolin), manure salt, kainit, nitrate of soda, ammonia liquor.

---

courtesy of the Lynn Museum, Norfolk Museums Service

During 1910 the head foreman, F.W Morgan died and A Durrant

was appointed assistant secretary. Tonnage of manure sold amounted to 34,560; an increase of 3,364 tons over 1909.

The works had, by this time, become a considerable undertaking as the photograph below illustrates. It was taken in 1910 and shows the old works, also known as A and B works.

acknowledgements the London and Provincial Magazine

In 1913 the directors received letters from two men on the works asking for an increase in wages. This did achieve a result in that the wages for a day labourer rose to 4.1/2d per hour, for a furnaceman to 32/6d per week and carpenters' wages increased by 1/2d per hour. A decision was also taken to have a messroom erected by Boulton and Paul.

At the outbreak of war in 1914, 32 men from the Company volunteered for service.

The first wartime problem was loss of Belgian phosphate which led to difficulties in making a 26% superphosphate. New customers had to be turned down because of shortages in labour, potash, bags and coal.

The directors sent one ton of manure to Belgian refugees at Littleport. They also insured the works against war damage. (The Board received information that an old liner was moored at the entrance to the Great Ouse in case of enemy action, in which case it would have been sunk to block the approaches).

THE FIRST VOLUNTEERS

Ainger, Bass, Bloom, Brown G.R, Clark, Clitheroe, Cooper, Edge, Fayers, Hardy, Hart, Harvey, Hendry, Hurn, Jarvis, Lynn, Manning, Mennell, Neale, Oakes, Parnell C, Parnell G, Peake, Petchey, Register, Russell, Shearman, Sheriff, Spaxman, Stinton, Suitor, Thurston.

Source: Lynn News and County Press, Saturday September 5th, 1914
courtesy of the Lynn News

During 1915 the Bucks Yeomanry took over the recently built messroom for two months at a rent of two guineas per week and acid was sold for munitions.

The government made WNF a 'controlled establishment' in 1916, one of the consequences being that a man had to be stationed by a telephone at night ready to receive notice of an impending air raid.

At about this time the Board made an observation that "there was a very large number of forms to be filled in for the government." They also requested a signal light on the Harbour Branch Railway to be extinguished after the last train, as it advertised the position of the works to a zeppelin.

Darkness, necessary as a defence measure against night time air raids, may have been a contributory cause in a fatal accident in 1916 involving John Robinson, a 65 year old nightwatchman who had charge of a boiler. Mr Robinson, who incurred a fractured skull, was found by Tom Taylor, a plumber, who had been "directing the watching of the outside premises of the Company." He had apparently fallen from the top of a boiler into an iron store, a distance of approximately 6 feet. Another witness at the inquest was furnaceman Alfred Dickerson.

An accident involving property occurred in the same year, when a WNF barge struck and damaged Stow bridge. The Company paid £125 compensation.

A Mr Hammond was called up and at the end of the year seven women were engaged (see chapter 6). A war bonus was paid and this was increased to 5/- per week for men and 2/6d for boys in 1917.

Shortage of pyrites meant that coke had to be used to keep the furnaces hot whilst waiting for supplies.

The war ended and in 1919 the men were paid at the full-time rate on Peace Celebration Saturday.

In 1920 Thomas Brown died in his 83rd year. In addition to his duties as managing director, a position he had relinquished only 6 weeks previously, he had been both a Borough and a County Councillor. He held several prominent positions in public life being the first chairman of the local education committee and occupying this post when the Duke of York (later to become King George V) opened the Technical School in the Hospital Walks, also when King Edward VII opened the Lynn Grammar School.

In the same year a new company was formed called the West Norfolk Farmers' Manure and Chemical Company (1920)Limited.

Thomas Brown
courtesy Mrs M Brown

The total revenue received in the 23 year life of the old Company was £3,950,612.2.3d from which £394,985.18.1d was declared as profit.

Again in 1920, the name of the company was changed to the West Norfolk Farmers' Manure and Chemical Co-operative Company Limited.

In 1922, a presentation was made to James Brown to mark 50 years of faithful service. Labourers' wages were £2.6.1d for a 47 hour week. In August of that year they were reduced to 40/- per week.

James Brown died in 1925 at the age of 78. Like his brother, he had played an important part in public affairs, being a member of the Lynn Board of Guardians. He was a churchwarden of All Saint's Church, Lynn, for 40 years. He was also associated with the Lynn Co-operative Society. His sons were Joe S. Brown (accountant) and H.H. Brown (Manager). A daughter, Edith, also occupied a position in the office.

Douglas H. Reid, son-in-law of Dr H.C Brown having married his daughter Enid, became the new Company secretary.

The 1920's saw the General Strike. The managing director issued a statement to the effect that if any employee went on strike he would not under any circumstances be re-employed. In the event, all employees remained loyal to the Company and did not join in and some offered their services to protect the works in case of trouble. Thirty served as special constables.

James Brown.
courtesy Lynn News

Sales of manures and straight fertilisers in 1926/27 totalled 46,603 tons.

The first mention of an employee retiring was in 1926 when Elizah Calton, aged 69, had to 'stand down' after 40 years service due to ill health.

Expansion in the 1930's included the acquisition of Marine Traders Ltd, setting up a new factory at Boston in Lincolnshire and building a factory at Flixborough, as a joint venture with Fisons.

In 1931 a pension was awarded to J. Skerritt (50 years service) due to health reasons. The following year, R.R. Hill was given a silver salver to mark 50 years service. He was told at the presentation that it was hoped he would remain in the Company's service for many years to come!

During the 30's, pensions were also awarded to T. Lake, F. Palmer, L. Stinton, H. Bass, A. Mitchell, S. Dyble, B. Fretwell, J. Turney, J. Adcock, H. Tice, G. Hardy, G. English and G. Riches. The amounts varied from 10/- to 15/- per week.

The Coronation year of 1937 was marked by the award of gratuities to employees of 7/6d to 10/- according to age.

Production of fertiliser in the 1936/37 season was nearly 56,000 tons of which nearly 86% was delivered by road.

The shadows of war had begun to gather. The Italian/Abyssinian conflict resulted in an increase in freight charges and the Spanish Civil War gave problems regarding the supply of some raw materials. As the second world war grew nearer, plans were made to erect shelters and to purchase respirators for employees in case of gas attack. Arrangements were also made for the works to be camouflaged. In early 1939, a works fire brigade was organised and plans made to build a fire station. Employees were encouraged to join the Territorial Army and were given full pay during training.

In 1939 the pay for labourers was 47/- per week of 47 hours. Men in charge of machines received an additional 2/-. The policy over wartime service was that wages were made up for married men and single men with dependants to the same amount as they received while employed by the Company. Single men without any dependants received an allowance of 10/- per week.

Tom Snape. "When war broke out the maintenance engineer, Reg Brown said to me, "Did you take your deferment papers with you?" When I said no, he said, "You silly young bugger. You'll be in the Army now."

I was called up into the army on 10/- a week and the firm made my money up to my rate at the time."

On November 16th, 1939, Dr Henry Charles Brown, the managing director died at the age of 77. He had taken an active part in the civic life of King's Lynn, being elected to the Council in 1898 as a representative of the south ward. He was appointed an alderman in 1922 and became the Mayor in 1936, Coronation year. He had been a deputy chairman of the Conservancy Board, a member of the Board of Governors of the grammar school and a churchwarden of All Saints Church.

Dr Brown was a Fellow of the Institute of Chemists, a United Kingdom representative of the International Superphosphate Association and a past president of the Fertiliser Manufacturers' Association. He was succeeded as managing director by his son, Mr Eric H.I. Brown, MA.

Earlier in the year, the death occurred of the chairman Mr A.H. Clarke at the age of 84. He joined the Board in 1897 and became chairman in 1926. He was succeeded by Mr S.A. Whittome of Ramsey.

Dr H.C. Brown
courtesy Mrs M Brown

Difficulty was experienced in obtaining sufficient, suitable men for both the Lynn and Boston works. The war also meant the loss of supplies of potash from Germany, one of the principal sources. Later, supplies of potash from France also stopped. The government gradually took over responsibility for the supply of raw materials. They also brought in price controls.

Bob Pinnock. "A number of Control of Fertiliser Orders were made to set the maximum prices which could be charged. This was the cash price ruling during the four months ending 30th June, 1939. All producers and distributors were required to register with the Ministry of Agriculture and Fisheries. Later restrictions were imposed on analyses of compounds and the size of packaging to be used."

North America was a major source of supply for raw materials. It was also a source of triple superphosphate. (By April, 1943, WNF had received 2,500 tons of this material).

In 1940, R.R. Hill was awarded a pension after 55 years service. J. Hildon, 40 years, and Mrs A.L. Catton, also received pensions. H.J. Fenn received a gold watch for 51 years service. A National Savings Group was started.

Fire watchers were placed on night duty using a 'spotters' tower alongside the River Nar, between the two works. During the daytime, as part of the ARP Regulations, 'lookouts' were posted so that work could be carried out during an alert.

Robert Thwaite. "My father, Walter Thwaite, worked on the Den. He lost an eye in an accident on the works. He was chipping some acidy material and a bit went into his eye and burnt it.

During the war he was in a spotters' post and put the siren on if he spotted enemy aircraft. I remember taking his Sunday dinner over to him."

An air raid on 13th November, 1940, resulted in a high explosive bomb dropping on the old works, causing some damage. A stick of ten H.E. bombs fell into a field alongside the new works.

In January, 1941, 3 incendiary bombs dropped on the works and were quickly extinguished. For this action the Works ARP section was praised by the authorities.

In February, 1941, the Company were informed by the Ministry of Labour that a considerable number of men would be called up in the near future. They also enquired as to whether female labour could be used.

Works A.R.P. Personnel. May, 1941.

Back Row, L to R, J. Royle, G. Jubey, W. Thwaite, F. Westmoreland, W. Suiter, F. Stokes, J. Gore, C. King, W. Jarvis, B. Riches, H. Dawson.
Second Row, F. Rust, A. Burrows, C. Manning, S. Bowman, F. Taylor, W. Bedwell, H. Fysh, H. Shaw, J. Groom, F. Lake, G. West, L. Cooke, T. Barrett.
Third Row, H. Hill, W. Ketteringham, E. Taylor, G. Watson, J. Shearman, G. Clitheroe, F. Dunbabin, B. Targett, W. Elms, W. Watson, L. Saunders, L. Linford, W. Vaughan.
Front Row, A. Taylor, F. Chatten, W. Barnaby, L. Rout, D.H. Reid (Sec. & General Manager), E.H.I. Brown (Managing Director), A.E. Brown, H.J. Fenn, R.H. Brown, T. Burrows, W. West, C. Sands, R. Castle, P. Marsters.

courtesy of the Lynn News

Pensions were given to George Laws, Jack West and S. Sheppardson (41 years service).

George Brown, the chief engineer died on 6.8.1941 after 37 years service. (His two sons on the works were Aubrey and Reg).

In 1942, the 12 hour working shift was reduced to one of 8 hours. Following a visit from H.M. Inspector of Factories, a works canteen was inaugurated, with a manageress. Due to lack of support the supply of hot meals was eventually discontinued. Crash shelters were erected and a section of the National Fire Service was established on the works. A social held in the works assembly hall raised £12 for parcels for employees who were prisoners of war.

Works A.R.P. Personnel. May, 1941.
courtesy of the Lynn News

In July, 1944, Mr J.S. Brown (son of James Brown) completed 54 years service and was presented with a silver salver.

More employees received pensions; these included R. Fayers, Walter Lake, G.W. Clitheroe (38 years service) T.W. Arrowsmith, F. Daisley, H.H. Brown (44 years service) J.W. Ashby (50 years service).

As the war in Europe came to an end thoughts returned to growth.

Bob Pinnock. "Following the 1939-1945 war, the directors agreed that major reconstruction and modernisation was required. It was estimated that this would cost in excess of one million pounds and that additional capital would have to be raised. Merchant bankers were asked to raise this capital in the city. Unfortunately, money was in great demand throughout the Country at this time for rebuilding industry and the Capital Issues Committee, who regulated the supply of money, vetoed the Company's application.

To obtain the funds required various persons were approached and eventually the Co-operative Wholesale Society agreed to help fund the rebuilding on certain conditions. The most onerous of these were:-

1   equal representation in the board room with the concession that 'local interest' would always provide the chairman, and,

2   an improved trade agreement between the CWS and WNF be entered into giving the CWS the right to sell 50% of the resulting increased production.

These agreements were completed and the CWS became a 50% holder of the Company in the Autumn of 1953."

On 2.11.1945, a decision was made that all employees would retire on reaching the age of 70, unless special circumstances and arrangements were made.

Mr J.S. Brown retired on 30.6.1946. Mr J.G. Newby was appointed as accountant with W. Baxter as assistant accountant.

The annual works outing, suspended during the war, was restarted.

On Friday 6th September, 1946, a 'welcome home' dance was held, funded by employees and the Company. It was noted that sixty ex-servicemen had now returned into the employ of the Company.

In 1947, A.E. Barron achieved 50 years service and the working week was altered. A five day week of 44 hours came into effect from 1.6.1947 to 30.11.1947 and a five and a half day week of 44 hours for the following six months.

Dan Rout received a gold watch in 1948 for 50 years service and a pension on retirement on 14.4.1952 having reached the age of 70. Other retirees during this time included W.F. Golden and B.M. Targett.

In the three month period December 1949 to February 1950, the Company lost three senior members of staff: A.C.K. Sheppard, who died in December, 1949 at the age of 66 had been associated with the Company for over 47 years. He had been the secretary and director of Boal Quay Wharfingers Ltd, a subsidiary company handling the importation of raw materials (see chapter 13). W.L. Hammond, died in January, 1950, during his 65th year, worked for the Company for over 47 years on the sales side of the business. L. Elms died in February 1950, at the age of 45. He had joined the office staff in 1918 and became head of the order and delivery department.

One of the highlights in the Company's history occurred in June, 1950, when for the first time a show stand, designed, constructed and erected by employees, was exhibited at the Royal Norfolk Show held at Anmer on the Royal Estate. On the second day of the two-day show, His Majesty King George VI visited the stand with Princess Margaret and the chairman, managing director and secretary of the Company were presented. The stand won the 'Barclay's Bank Challenge Cup' which was presented by the King to Mr Eric Brown.

Just over one year later, tragedy struck. On Sunday, 26th August, 1951, Mr Eric Henry Ibbetson Brown, the managing director of the Company, died while playing cricket at the age of 47.

Anthony Avis. "I knew Eric well, as he founded and ran a cricket team on the sports ground behind the works in which I played in the immediate post war period. He had just done a spell of bowling and had given me the ball to follow him when he suddenly collapsed and I with other players, supported him on the field."

Mr E.H.I. Brown.
courtesy Mrs M Brown

A week earlier, Mr Eric Brown had accompanied the works football team to play a return match with the Standaert Fertiliser Company team in Belgium. The Belgian players had visited and played the WNF side in the Spring as a part of the Festival of Britain celebrations.

He had been a chairman of Lynn Conservancy Board, chairman of King's Lynn Port Users' Association and a member of Council and a past president of the Fertiliser Manufacturers' Association.

Mr Eric Brown made a point of knowing the christian names of employees, several hundred of whom attended his funeral and followed behind two of the Company's lorries which had been decked out with wreaths. To them, he was always known as ' Mr Eric' as his father before him had been 'Dr Harry.'

Following the death of the managing director, Mr D.H. Reid remained in the position of general manager and Mr A.I. Coleman was brought in as deputy general manager. Eventually, they were appointed joint general managers.

In 1955 another highlight occurred when the Company was appointed a Royal Warrant Holder.

During the 1950's, the retirement age came down to 65. A.W. Abel retired in 1955 and in 1958 one lady and 23 men retired and were presented with awards by the chairman, T. Allen Ringer, at a special ceremony.

Awards were made to Edgar Broad (54 years), W. Cox (53 years), J.W. Fysh (52 years), W.L. Petchey (50 years), A.Mitchell (48 years), F. Taylor (47 years), G.W. Reeve (45 years), T. Bennington (44 years), H. Bocking (41 years), A.E. Hickman (37 years), A.E. Hudson (33 years), M. Chase (30 years), W.W. Nicholls (26 years), W.G. Claydon (23 years), A.J. Mawby (19 years), A.G. Fisher (18 years), W.J. Catton (17 years), A.E. Easton (17 years), H. Hooks (17 years), Mrs Burton (16 years), J.C. Hovell (14 years), A. Edwards (12 years), R. Peake (12 years) and S.J. Goodson (10 years).

In 1959, Mr T Allen Ringer retired after 14 years service as chairman of the Company and 20 years on the Board of Directors. Mr G.A. Worth succeeded him, (as chairman).

Retirement ceremony: (L to R) T. Allen Ringer, W.L. Petchey, J.W. Fysh, W. Cox, Edgar Broad.
courtesy of the Lynn News

Mr Douglas Reid resigned as joint general manager in 1961 and became a director. A.I. Coleman was appointed to the position of general manager. The following year the title was changed to that of chief executive director and a management team was formed which consisted of A.I. Coleman, J.G. Newby (secretary and executive director) P. Craven, R.P. Libbey, who retired the following year, H.C. Kidd and P.J. McHale, all designated as executive directors.

In 1962 the name of the Company was changed to West Norfolk Fertilisers Limited. (They were still a farmers' co-operative).

A.I. Coleman resigned from the Company in 1964 and his place was taken by P.J. McHale.

The Royal Norfolk Show, Anmer, June 1950.
courtesy of R Goodchild

The Royal visit to the show stand.   June, 1950.
courtesy of R Goodchild

Chapter 4

THE TAR WORKS

From the earliest days the Company was producing organic chemicals from coal tar. The tar works was situated between the River Nar and the harbour branch railway line, approximately 100 yards south of the Wisbech Road in South Lynn.

The main source of supply was Cambridge Gas Works, who also supplied ammoniacal gas liquor which was used to make sulphate of ammonia. These materials were brought to South Lynn by barge.

Les Figgis. "They used to bring barges down the River Great Ouse from Cambridge and Ely and then come down the Nar turning in at Paul's Mill. Because the steam tug couldn't get under the gas works bridge, two men brought each barge down to the works using long poles. They pushed these down into the mud and walked along the barge deck as it was poled along."

Typically, a tug would pull two specially made tank barges, one containing tar, the other ammoniacal liquor.

Horses were probably used to pull the barges at some period. Dorothy Palmer, daughter of an early employee, Walter Palmer, remembers being told that when a horse-drawn barge reached the gas works bridge, the horse would be uncoupled and while the barge man was poling the barge under the bridge, the horse would dutifully jump over the fence, cross the road and jump over the fence on the other side and wait to be recoupled to the barge.

On arrival at the tar works, the barges were secured to jetties and discharged by steam-driven pumps. The ammoniacal gas liquor was converted into crystals of sulphate of ammonia by reacting the ammonia gas with sulphuric acid. The coal tar was piped to large stills, or retorts, and heated.

As the tar became gradually hotter, the various components were separated by a process known as fractional distillation where the oil with the lowest boiling point distils off first, followed progressively by heavier oils with higher boiling points, each being collected in individual iron tanks. Eventually nothing would be left in the still but a residue called pitch. This would be allowed to run out of the bottom of the still, while still hot and in a molten state, into a large open pitch lake or beck and allowed to set.

Battery of stills, 1910, showing part of pitch lake or beck.
acknowledgements The London & Provincial Magazine

Les Figgis. "One thing I remember was that there used to be a large pit full of black pitch that gave off vapours. Children used to be brought by their mothers and stand by this pit to breathe the vapours. I assumed they had some chest complaint but I didn't know whether or not it was on medical advice."

One lady, who still lives in South Lynn, remembers when she was six years old being held up by her mother at the side of the pitch lake to breathe the vapours, in order to cure her whooping cough.

When the pitch was cold, it would be broken up and loaded into wagons to be sold, probably for use in road making. Pitch from the tar works was sold as far away as Antwerp in Belgium.

Leonard Smith. "One of the worst piece-rate jobs you could be put on was breaking up the pitch bed. It used to set hard like toffee, about three to four inches thick. We broke it up with sledge hammers, starting at the outside and gradually nibbling away at the pitch towards the centre. The work was hard but the worst part was the fumes that made your eyes intensively painful for several days. Some of the men made eyeshields out of plywood, putting in pinholes so that they could see what they were doing. After it was broken up, the slabs of pitch were carried in big metal containers with handles and loaded into rail wagons."

Gradually more additions were made to the battery of stills and 'residuals' and 'gas liquor' were being purchased from nearly thirty individual gas companies, including Cambridge, Ely, Bedford, Downham Market, Hunstanton and King's Lynn.

The tar works, 1910, showing stills.
acknowledgements The London & Provincial Magazine

A fire occurred in the tar works on Saturday May 13th, 1876, when a tar still boiled over and the vapours ignited, causing a fire which spread to other tanks. The fire produced a dense cloud of black smoke which was visible from several miles away. The manager and men who were on duty managed to save most of the contents of a tank full of creosote, but despite their efforts approximately 3000 gallons of distilled tar oils were destroyed by the fire.

The Lynn fire engines were set to work cooling the still and other tanks and were assisted by a small fire engine belonging to the Great Eastern Railway Company at Lynn station.

According to a report in the Lynn News and County Press, a large number of people gained access to the works to see the fire but they were removed when a contingent of police officers arrived under the charge of Supt. Ware.

At a later date, a steam pump was purchased to provide water in case of fire.

In 1890, the Company were paying 25/- a ton for tar and distilling this to obtain products such as anthracene, carbolic acid, cresylic acid, creosote and creosote salts, black varnish, naphtha, light oil, green oil, grease oil and pyridine. In 1899, black varnish was offered at 12/6d per 40 gallon barrel for preserving wood or ironwork. During the first world war, the Company was manufacturing refined tar for the various road authorities in the distict.

Following an increase in the price of casks or barrels used to ship products, the Company employed a cooper, Mr J. Appleton.

A recipe which they gave for the treatment of wireworm was a mixture of wood sawdust saturated with creosote (other coal tar products were also used). The principle was that when the saturated sawdust was ploughed into the soil, the warm ground would cause the creosote to vaporise and result in the wireworm travelling to the surface, there to be consumed by birds. (An early attempt to use a 'natural' pesticide).

Derek Foreman. "In the 1930's, the Company was still selling
    barrels of tar varnish (also known as black varnish) and creosote.
    People used to come in with their containers and buy one or two
    gallons of creosote."

Bill Fawkes. "The tar varnish produced in the tar works was much favoured by North End fishermen for their smacks. When the tar varnish dried it had a glossy sheen and used to shine like varnish."

Over a period of time several wooden steam tug - boats came into use. These included the 'Annie' (she had a new hull built by Worfolk Brothers in 1910), the 'Nellie' (sank at the mouth of the Great Ouse in 1917 and subsequently raised and repaired) and the steel tug, the 'Olga' (named after one of Dr Harry Brown's daughters). The 'Olga' was skippered by Captain Jack Lee.

Les Figgis. "One of my jobs was cleaning out the boiler on the little tug. I was the smallest and the only one who could crawl through the tubes. I remember going into the boiler one day and the man in charge calling down to me, "The last man to do that had a fit you know!"

In 1928 there were signs that the tar works was starting to become unprofitable and production ceased in the 1930's. Tank barges DC19 and 10A were sold in 1939 and a remaining tug and barge sold to the Peterborough Shipping Company Ltd.

In 1940, a decision was taken that the tar works would be dismantled and sold as labour became available.

Chapter 5

WORK ON THE FLOORS

All manure produce by the firm was in powdered form from 1872 to 1945 when the first granulation plant came into operation. The sale of granular fertiliser did not begin to exceed that of the powder variety until early in the 1950's when the much larger second granulation plant came on stream at the new works. Some powdered manure was still being produced in the 1960's.

The 'floors' relate to the various warehouses and sheds where the manure was stored and prepared for bagging and loading. These included Black Shed and Kerkham's Warehouse (the spelling in some documents is 'Kirkham's') at the old works and A, B and C floors, New Shed (built 1926) and River Shed, all at the new works.

Gradually WNF extended their range of manures. In 1890 they were advertising in the Lynn News and County Press, "any special mixture prepared with care" In 1895, they agreed to make "any manure containing any percentage that dealers may require."

Two examples taken from a 1901 fertiliser recipe book show that they were formulating special manures for individual farmers.

FERTILISER RECIPE BOOK				
Oat Manure for W Heading.	T -	C	Mustard Manure for Hobson. T -	C
Supers 25/28%	11	5	Supers 32/34% 3	5
Flights		10	Bone flour	10
Bone flour	1	0	N/Soda	15
Nitre	5	15	Kainit	10
	18	10	5	0

courtesy of Norfolk Record Office

For the men who laboured on the floors the work was always hard, dirty, dusty and sometimes hazardous. Most of the bagging, loading and dispatch activity was crammed into three short, hectic months from about the middle of January until the middle of April, with many of the men being hired just for that season. The work would be carried out by organised gangs consisting normally of four men to a gang. These men stayed together and would form highly skilled working groups.

Leonard Smith. "All gangwork was on piecework and you had to work like hell. When you were put on piecework you handed in your check (a washer with a hole in the middle), I was check number 266. The piecework rate started the moment you handed it in. If you got taken off piecework you went to the office and got your check back. If some one in your gang was late, you all waited ten minutes to see if he was coming in. After 15 minutes the man late was automatically put on the check rate and they put another man in the gang."

The type of work carried out on the floors is detailed in three notebooks left by Claude Riches, a former WNF employee. The neat methodical entries are believed to have been made by his father, George Riches, who kept a working diary of what he did every day and the varying piecework rates which were shared between the four members of the gang. (The names Reeve and Gathercole are mentioned and may have been members of the gang). He also kept a running total of his wages which he totalled annually. The notebooks cover the period 1915-1923. It is interesting to note that during this period no holidays were taken and a six day week was worked with an occasional Sunday and Christmas Day and Boxing Day were the only days off.

courtesy Mrs Beatrice Flint (nee Riches)

Bill Fawkes. "In order to make manure ready for bagging up, a bed of supers was first spread on the floor. This was known as 'laying down.' On top of this, salts such as muriate of potash and sulphate of ammonia were spread. You then turned it over with shovels once or twice to make sure it was all well mixed."

Screening followed next.

Leonard Smith. "When I started at WNF in 1926, I was put in a bagging gang with Claude Riches, Stan Say and 'young' Pat Bramham. We were called the second gang. Our first job was screening supers. A big screen, about six to eight feet long and about five feet wide with wooden sides and metal mesh (approximately 1/4" screen size) was propped up and two members of the gang shovelled supers against the front of the screen. The material that wouldn't go through the screen rolled down onto the floor and it was broken up with the back of a shovel. Bertie Fenn, the foreman, used to walk round the floor to see that you weren't putting any of the 'hardcore' behind the screen. (The farmers didn't like this oversize material because it used to block up their machines)."

Bill Fawkes. "The real rough stuff was thrown back onto the main heap, to be broken up by the 'breaker', which was the first of the bagging machines. The gang then bagged up the manure. We used a set of the 'crash-bang' scales. One man held a sack on the scales while two filled it with shovels. When it was full (16 stones) they used a short 'hicking' stick under the bag to lift it onto the top of the scales. After being stitched up, the 'carrier away' got it onto his shoulders and took it away. The sack needle used to stitch up bags was approximately nine inches long and had a blade like a knife."

W.J. Howlett. "Some of the bag stitchers were always playing practical jokes. If you weren't careful you walked away with your trousers attached to a sack of manure - someone had stitched your trousers to it!"

There was also a serious side to bag stitching. An employee, William Rose, lost an eye in May 1904. Apparently while Mr Rose was holding a sack, the man stitching it up accidentally punctured his eye with the needle.

Leonard Smith. "I went on sewing up bags in my first year and remember when I stitched myself up. We had been loading a truck using a wooden plank. I had the needle ready in my hand when somebody moved the plank out of my way. The end of the plank struck my needle and it went into my leg and out the other side. Charley Beevus was the foreman and when I told him what I had done he said "I'll pull it out for you." He then went to the office and got some iodine to put on it. I was back to work as usual the next day!"

When manure, such as superphosphate, was made and tipped to form a large heap on the floor, it would remain there until the start of the next season. By this time it would be rock hard and would have to be picked down manually. This was very hard work and also hazardous because in order to get the vertical face of the heap to collapse, an overhang would have to be created across the face by undermining the base of the heap with a pick and shovel, using a shovel with an eight foot handle where necessary. The sides would then be cut away so as to make part of the heap fall. Occasionally long iron bars would have to be hammered in to make this happen.

In 1923, an employee, Albert Charles Ives, one of a gang of four men, was buried in a fall of about twenty to twenty-five tons of manure. Strenuous efforts to dig him out were made by his comrades (two of whom were named at the inquest as Percy Yates and Harry Frost). Unfortunately, Mr Ives died in the West Norfolk and Lynn hospital on the following day.

The gradual introduction of mechanisation reduced the risk of heap falls but never completely eliminated them.

Bill Fawkes. "I started at the new works when I was 16, driving a small bagging machine for 16/10d a week. A gang of men worked with this machine picking down manure from the heap and shovelling it into the hopper of the machine. The manure was broken up by a power-driven wheel containing spikes and went into another hopper from where it was bagged up."

This small machine may have been the forerunner of the so-called "German" machine or "Lanvermeyer".

The first Lanvermeyer excavating and bagging machine was purchased in 1925 and is believed to have been the first such machine purchased in this country. A German mechanic came over to help install the machine and impressed the WNF management as being a very versatile man able to function as a fitter, blacksmith and carpenter.

Bill Fawkes. "Part of the wall of Kerkham's warehouse (facing the tar works) had to be knocked down to get the machine on to the floor."

Les Figgis. "The Lanvermeyer had three or four parallel and vertical looped chains in front to which were fixed sets of cups. The machine was driven by electrical power and had wheels in front. As the machine moved forward the cups started to eat into the vertical face of the heap. There were also sets of knives that went up and down behind the cups and broke up the supers. The material was conveyed by the cups to a hopper, then to a screen which was shaken by rocking arms. The dust went through to be bagged up at 3 or 4 filling spouts and the oversize went back through the crushing system."

Bill Fawkes. "There was also a manually operated lever which controlled the rate of the cut. I had to go under the machine while it was moving, to keep the floor clean and level. This was important otherwise the machine would start to climb and the cups wouldn't cut into the heap."

Because the first Lanvermeyer was successful, two more machines were purchased in 1926.

The machines were working in Kerkhams, in Black Shed and New Shed with Dave Jary and Fred Say, followed by Fred Smith, and Walter "Wacker" West in charge of them respectively.

When the material in the heap got too hard for the Lanvermeyer machines to dig out, the 'blower-up' or blaster would be called to demolish the face of the heap.

Bill Fawkes. "When I first started, the 'blasters' were Fred Taylor, Bill Clitheroe, (later to become senior foreman at the old works) and Jimmy Rust."

Les Figgis. "A 10 foot bar was knocked into the heap, then it was tapped and pulled out. Two or three explosive cartridges would then be pushed in with a wooden rod. The waxed covering on the last cartridge would be opened at the end and a detonator, previously secured to a length of fuse with a special crimping tool would be pushed into the cartridge and the covering replaced. The hole was then tamped or plugged, the fuse lit and everybody stood well back. There would be a loud bang and the face of the heap would be brought down."

Later the blasters were Harry Massen, Pat Bramham and Harry Barker. The explosive cartridges, detonators and fuses were collected from a concrete explosive store surrounded by a blast wall. The store was licensed and well-separated from other buildings. The cartridges and detonators were kept segregated in a wooden container fitted with a lid and leather carrying strap, known as the 'ferret box.'

Also operating as bagging machines were the pulvers which were in fixed positions. Two were located in River Shed and one in Black Shed.

Bill Fawkes. "They were supplied by electric tram skips which discharged into a chute fitted with bars at floor level. An elevator fed the manure into a top hopper where it fell onto a rotating wheel of knives. From there it was thrown onto a deflector plate then via screens into two hoppers from where it was bagged up."

W.J. Howlett. "The pulver at Black Shed was operated by Lew Berry. It had a type of starter that had to be wound up slowly so that the pulver was gradually brought up to speed. If it was wound up too quickly the belts would fly off."

Eddy Betts. "In 1936 I was put in charge of one of the pulvers on River Shed. The one at the top end was fed by electric trams filled by an electric digger shovel which was operated by Percy Marsters and Sammy Stinton. The pulver at the bottom end was fed by tram and a Fordson tractor shovel. I believe a George Hammond was in charge of the first River Shed pulver He was followed by Wally Green. Some of the Fordson tractor drivers during my time on River Shed were Bernard Gathercole, Freddy Westmoreland and Fred Taylor. The rate for working the pulver was 2d per ton on a piecework basis. The other men in the gang got less. The pulver produced about 80-100 tons a day of powdered manure. It was a rotten job. The dust used to fly up in a great cloud everytime you tipped a tram load of manure and let it go. You wore a handkerchief over your mouth and nose, even so the dust got into your mouth, up your nose and into your eyes. The dust used to build-up in front of the pulver and got compacted down by the tram wheels. This had to be chipped away at the end of the day; sometimes it would be about 9" thick. If the pulver broke down and the cause was not your fault, you got one hours pay. For example, if a belt broke and had to be repaired by either George Lake or Joe Mitchell."

The introduction of the power-driven dry mixing plants at both the old and the new works removed some of the more strenuous work, but hand mixing was still used for some special manures. These were handled by the 'heavy gang', so called because it involved heavy manual work.

The manure was tipped on the various floors by trams that ran on an overhead rail. These were pushed and tipped manually by both men and women.

Tom Snape. "When I joined in 1938, I first worked on the tram road pushing trams full of fertiliser up above the shed floor, tipping then returning with the empty tram, and so on."

Les Figgis. "There was a knack in tipping a tram. You had to swing the tram sideways and at the same time release a catch which made the tram swing upside down and tip its load."

W.J.Howlett. "When I started work at WNF in 1935 for 23/8d per week, the working routine was one week on the dry mixer, one week on the old works tramroad and one week in Kerkham's warehouse on piecework, which was 1d a ton. There was always a friendly atmosphere and I enjoyed working there, although there was no such thing as a clean job.

As lads up on the tramroad, we would fill a bag with the last material, called 'flights'. It mainly consisted of air. We would then drop it on some one below. One day I did this and I accidentally hit the foreman, H.H. Brown, known as 'Tuffin' Brown. He used to walk round, then suddenly he would stop and sniff. "Somebody's been smoking woodbines" he would say.

Smoking was forbidden, but eventually it was relaxed because so many people were going off to smoke in the toilet. This was alongside the Nar and consisted of a long board that could accommodate ten to twelve men at a time."

Les Figgis. "Our toilets were on the river bank and were three to four feet high on staging. There was a gap under the doors so that the foreman could see if there was anyone in there. One day he was flabbergasted to see cigarette smoke coming out of the top but apparently no men were occupying the toilets; the men inside had lifted their feet up above the gap in the door."

George Palmer. "I began work (clock no.124) as most people did to start with, on the old works dry mixing unit on 22nd January, 1946. My job was to bag up sulphate of ammonia in 16 stone hessian sacks. Someone else took them away on a sack barrow to a grating by the mixing unit. The man in charge was 'Arnt' Wright; it was known as being 'on the handle.' The handle controlled the flow of supers into the batch being weighed. At a signal from 'Arnt', the sulphate of ammonia was tipped as were bags of muriate of potash or sulphate.

There would be a total of six men on the dry mixer. In addition to 'Arnt' and myself, someone would be running in potash. This had to be broken up by a man wielding a 14lb hammer so that it would go through the grating. Another man would be running in filler, already bagged. This would either be powder from ground cocoa or sunflower husks. 'Arnt' used to roll his own cigarettes using the cocoa husks and the smell was awful!

Two men would be in the supers silo, which was cone shaped, trimming the solid superphosphate down with picks on to a moving conveyor at the bottom of the silo.

The muriate of potash came in rail wagons, ready bagged. The wagons would be parked in the rail siding adjacent to Kerkham's warehouse. The doors of the wagon would be opened and a set of planks put down."

Bill Fawkes. "I spent some time with the heavy gang who used to offload the rail wagons. After the planks were put down the 16 stone bags were carried off. You actually trotted along the planks with a bag on your back and they bounced up and down as you went along them. I 'ran' with Percy Allen and we timed the rhythm of the boards and this made it easier to carry."

By this time a ropeway had been installed to carry material to Kerkham's warehouse. This consisted of an endless wire rope to which the trams were clipped. The ropes pulled the full trams to the tipping point where a fixed 'striker' would cause them to swing upside down and discharge their contents and at the same time become detached from the moving wire rope. Occasionally the wire rope would break and would have to be quickly repaired.

Eddy Betts. "When New Shed was built, supers was supplied to it by an overhead belt conveyor to a ropeway. In charge of the New Shed ropeway was Ernie (Duke) Woodhouse. Jim (Chicken) Rose was the foreman."

In 1937, a unique automatic electric telpher tram system by Bleichert Mitchell Ltd was installed to supply manure to the Black Shed at the old works. Each tram held about half a ton of manure and was driven on a complex mono-rail system by its own electric motor which picked up current from overhead wires. To ensure that trams could not collide, switching stations were introduced in the electricity supply. As a tram passed a station it shut off the power to the section it had just left and switched it on again after it had passed through the next section.

When a tram hit a 'striker', mechanical linkage would cause the bottom of the tram to open and the load of manure to be discharged.

The telpher system was successful and in 1938 a decision was made for a telpher system to be installed at the new works to supply River Shed.

Interior of one of the sheds, 1932. On the right is a Lanvermeyer -these machines were in use until about 1950.

acknowledgements Town and Country News

The bags used on the floors were mainly 16 stone and made of hessian (jute). Later some 12 stone bags were introduced following requests from farmers.

Reg Rout. "I worked for a time bagging up supers and compounds in 16 stone bags. You hung the bags onto the 'German' machine until they were full. You then weighed them on the scales. Some of the men were very accurate in their estimation and could get the weight 'spot on.'"

Peter Barber. "I worked on the floors after returning after the war in 1946. Bill Vaughan, who was the foreman on River Shed at the time, used to come round and check weigh the bags. If we were filling 12 stone bags he would call me over to stand on one side of the scales (I weighed exactly 12 stones) while the sack to be check weighed would be placed on the other side. If we were on the 16 stone sacks, 'China' Clark would be used as a check weight because he weighed exactly 16 stones."

A break from one of the floors, circa 1932.

Back row: (L to R) Les Hornigold, Frank Bramham, Jack (Smacky) Greenacre, ? Rust, Bernard Gathercole, Eddy Betts, Front row: Jack Manning, Charley Ashby, Joe Mitchell, Dick Eglen.

courtesy of E Betts

All the bags were printed within the works.

Les Figgis. "After leaving the manure side I went into the bagroom, printing hessian sacks. It was all manual. I had a copper lid with the firm's name printed on a block underneath. I dipped this in a tray of ink and stamped a sack. You pulled this out of the way, dipped the printing block and stamped again; dip, stamp, pull; dip stamp, pull, and so on. I started in the baghouse under a Jack Hardy, who also used to splice ropes.

Eventually a printing machine was installed. This consisted of a roller drum on which was fixed a gelatine printing block. I was in charge of the bagroom by this time; a Thomas Ford-Smith also worked there. Some farmer's names were also printed on the sacks for example, A.H. Thompson, Symingtons, etc.

We used to store the sacks on an overhead floor and move them over a wooded slatted floor with a one-wheeled barrow. The telpher trams were running at the time so you had to watch out. One day the whole floor collapsed under the weight of the stack of sacks and big heavy beams came down. Fortunately, no one was injured because it happened at the weekend. As a result of this accident, the bagroom moved to South Lynn into a shed adjacent to the sports ground.

At the end of the season, the ends of my fingers were raw due to the continuous handling of sacks."

The printed sacks were taken to the various floors by the bagboy.

Alf Needham. "This was my first job with WNF. I started in 1946 as a bagboy at £2.10.0 per week. I carted the bags to the floors and sheds using a trailer and the 'Imp' tractor."

Chapter 6

WOMEN IN THE WORKS

The first women manual workers joined the firm in 1916, during the first world war when seven ladies were engaged. Unfortunately their names are not known by the author.

In 1917 a letter was received from the Ministry of Munitions suggesting that women should replace men picking down manure and feeding the bagging machine. The directors of WNF agreed that this was quite unsuitable work for women to undertake.

This photograph was taken in about 1918. The young ladies in the traditional brown overalls and headgear are (from left to right) Maude Howling, Mary Jary and Dolly Peck. Mary Jary later married WNF employee Claude Riches.

Women and girls carried out a variety of jobs at the works. They pushed and tipped trams containing about half a ton of manure. The tramroad had a slatted wooden floor and this apparently played havoc with their feet. They also cleaned and repaired sacks that had been returned by farmers.

Courtesy of Mrs Beatrice Flint

Leonard Smith. "Girls also took the bags away from the back of the 'German' machine (Lanvermeyer). They had great old wooden sack barrows to do the job with. They weren't like the modern day sack barrows with rubber tyres and wheel bearings but had big cast-iron wheels with no bearings. The wheels used to wobble about and the uneven floor made the work even harder for them and remember they were handling 16 stone bags!

The girls used to take turns sewing up the full bags. One girl would take a hank of the thick string over her shoulder and with a sack needle would stitch up a bag like lightning leaving two 'ears' standing up."

In 1940, during the second world war, WNF had difficulty in obtaining sufficient numbers of suitable men to ensure full production and dispatch. In the early part of 1941, a communication from the Ministry of Labour indicated that a considerable number of men would be called up in the near future and enquired whether more female labour could be utilised.

Many of the mens' wives, sisters and daughters worked there.

Alice Rockett, who became Mrs Spinks, was a forewoman on the tramroad during the war.

After the war, Alice was the canteen manageress and also worked with Mrs Nellie Lake and other ladies, making protective clothing for the men. This consisted of trousers and jackets made of hessian sacking stitched up on sewing machines. These 'suits' were used for dirty jobs and up to the late 1950's were the only protective clothing available.

> **SOME OF THE WOMEN IN THE WORKS:**
>
> Doris Clark, Maisie Collison, Milly Collison, Vera Dent, Dora, Violet and Lily Howlett, Maude Howling, Mary Jary, Molly Ludkin, Maisie Lyon, Edie Massen, Mrs E Needham, Florrie Oakes, Dolly Peck, Alice and Lily Rockett.

While in charge of the canteen, Alice used to go to great lengths to ensure that everyone received their fair share of tea and sugar during the rationing period. She would carefully measure out the tea and sugar for each shift with a teaspoon and then mix the two together! This mixture was put in a paper bag and made into a small parcel with newspaper and a sticky label attached, on which she wrote the shift and name of the plant or department. If you didn't take sugar in your tea, that was your hard luck!

Alice Rockett with a group of workers circa 1932.
courtesy of E Betts

Chapter 7

THE DENS

Phosphorus is one of the three main plant foods and the various substances sold by WNF as a source of this essential element included 'guano' (solidified bird-droppings from Peru), dissolved animal bones, bone meal and bone flour. basic slag (a bye-product from steelworks) and finely ground 'coprolite' (a form of fossilised animal dung which was dug out from deposits found in the Fens in the 19th century). Superphosphate was also sold.

The discovery that a mixture of sulphuric acid and mineral phosphate rock (sometimes called 'apatite') would result in a more soluble and therefore more beneficial plant food had been discovered some 30 years before WNF was founded. This compound was known as superphosphate of lime, 'supers' for short.

WNF imported the mineral phosphate from all over the world to make superphosphate. It varied in grade, according to location and also in colour, from the greyish-black Gafsa phosphate to the light ochre colouring of the phosphates from Morocco and Nauru Island. Although received in a fairly fine condition, phosphates first had to be ground to a fine powder in a mill.

The plant in which supers was made was always referred to as a 'den.' In the first dens the hot steaming and acidic material had to be dug out by the men with shovels and carried out in skep baskets. In 1915, the piecework rate for doing this hard and unpleasant job was 7d per ton dug, shared between the four men in the gang.

The first mechanical den was installed in the old works around 1919. Called the 'milch' den, the solid superphosphate was cut out using a power-driven propeller-like knife.

Bill Fawkes. "I worked on the old works den part time. In charge of the operation at that time was Harry Bass, who made the supers. 'Snowy' Palmer was the phosphate weigher and Harry Fysh and Jim Fysh looked after the den underneath.

The den was a horizontal cylinder with wheels underneath that ran on rails. When the den was full it was allowed to set, then hinged, curved doors, underneath, were released by pulling out a pin - when I worked there, that was my job.

One day the pin was taken out and the den hadn't set properly with a result that about twenty tons of very hot molten, slurry-like material gushed out. It was also still acidic. Everyone made a run for it but Jim Fysh caught his shoulder on one of the hanging doors and fell, straight into it. I believe he was scarred for a long time; his skin went a brownish colour afterwards.

Two heavy screws pulled the den slowly into a rotating knife that cut out the solid material."

A type of mechanical den was also installed at the new works. The power source for the equipment in the early days was steam, the steam raising boilers being installed at both the old and new works.

Les Figgis. "A huge flywheel drove a shaft that went across the yard to the mill and den. Although this had stopped when I was there, the equipment was still in the power station."

Generators were installed around 1921 to produce electrical power from the steam raising plant. A single large motor drove all the den and mill equipment via a system of belts, pulleys and shafting. Although it was dismantled in the second world war to make way for a more modern den, quite a lot is known regarding how it worked.

Les Figgis. "I left school at the age of 14, in 1924 on the Friday and started work at WNF on the Monday, still in short trousers, much to the amusement of the women workers!

My first job was on the top floor of the new works den. The day began at 6am and I walked through the allotments to Saddlebow Road. I had half an hour break at 7.30am. Then I worked 8-12 and 1-5, a 5.1/2 day week for which I received 10/-. Sometimes there was overtime.

The job consisted of manually weighing half a ton of phosphate rock into a mixer by pulling out and pushing in a metal slide. It was very dusty work. Everytime you pulled the slide, a cloud of phosphate dust came out and covered you from head to foot. I used to wear a sack hood over my head. When I walked home I left a trail of white footprints.

There was no telephone. Communication was by means of a vertical pipe that went all the way down to the man who operated the phosphate silo on the ground floor. I tapped once to tell him to start running phosphate. Two taps meant a little more and a little tune, 'bum-diddle-bum-bum' meant finish."

Reg Rout. "Occasionally there was spillage of the ground phosphate. When this happened it used to run down the phosphate elevator like water and nothing could stop it. It was called a 'woodruffer' when such an incident occurred, after an unfortunate man called Woodruff who was nearly buried by a fall of phosphate when he was the phosphate runner."

Les Figgis. "A man called Stinton weighed in half a ton of acid. The acid was blown up to the top of the den building by compressed air. The ground floor pumphouse was always known as 'Stintons.'

Fred Skippon was in charge of the den operation. One ton batches were run in from the mixer to the den below. This was a long horizontal tub with concrete walls. It had a wooden plate with four long screws at one end and an iron door at the other. When the den was full (about thirty tons) it was allowed to set. At the right time, the iron door at the front was opened and the four long screws began to push the material out of the den into a set of revolving metal rods that had 'stars' on their ends. These 'stars' cut out the supers which dropped onto a metal tray conveyor. The supers was then taken to a rasp which had knives to cut up the material.

Eventually I was given the job of looking after the rasp and my pay went up to 12/- per week. I had to use a long 8 foot shovel to keep the knives clear. Occasionally the shovel would touch the moving metal knives and it felt just like an electric shock.

When the material left the rasp it was blown by a fan into one of two silos; each held three dens, about ninety tons. From the silos it was picked down and conveyed to the tramroad and from there to the floors."

Cecil Sands. "One of my memories is seeing Biddy White picking down hot supers in the silo, with sacking wrapped round his legs to protect himself."

Les Figgis. "After the rasp job, I moved onto the 'stars' on the den. I used a 12 foot shovel to cut out the material that the 'stars' missed. My wages went up to 14/- a week."

In 1940/41, a new den was brought into operation to replace the 'stars' den at the new works. Called the Moritz Standaert den, it was a continuous operation and produced about 15 tons per hour. The den, which was shaped like a vertical cylinder with a truncated-cone bottom section, revolved slowly on trunnions. An internal rotating excavator, in a fixed position, cut out the solid supers onto a metal tray conveyor below.

Eric Broad. "The new works den operators when I joined the firm in 1946, were Fred Skippon, Joe Mawby and Stan Say (known as the 'Sergeant Major'). The old works den operator was Harry Fysh and the old works phosphate miller was Dave Spaxman."

Reg Rout. "The new works Moritz den occasionally used to 'run-out.' The den held thirty tons when full and the den operator mixed in to it to form a wall. Gradually the supers would be built up inside the den, still in a semi-liquid state. On rare occasions, the wall inside would collapse and the contents of the den would run out onto the tray conveyor underneath. It would be in a very hot and acidic state and the tray attendant would have to beat a hasty retreat."

Mancell Ryan. "I started on the new works den in about 1960, working on the tray conveyor and the other conveyors, taking the supers to either the tramroad or to the ropeway and new shed. On my shift Harry Fysh was on the mixer (the den at the old works had closed down by this time), Siddy Booer was the phosphate runner and Johnny Ward and Herbie Knowles were on the tramroad or ropeway.

I remember you had to run out of the way quickly if there was a run-out from the den; it used to pour down like hot slurry. There was a concrete wall at the back of the tray conveyor which meant there was only one way out, if you were unlucky enough to be working at that end."

The dens were usually shut-down during the summer months for annual maintenance.

Les Figgis. "As the smallest boy, in addition to cleaning the tug boiler, I and Sammy Stinton used to clean and tar varnish the inside of the condensers and scrubbers on the den (these had water sprays inside to knock-down and prevent noxious gases from the den process getting into the atmosphere).

We used to collect the tar varnish from the tar works in a bucket and it would still be warm. The tarring would be done off a boatswain's chair and you lowered yourself down the inside of the scrubber from the top. This job qualified for 'black money.'"

Chapter 8

THE ACID PLANTS

WNF manufactured sulphuric acid throughout its history to make superphosphate of lime and additionally, from the 1950's, phosphoric acid.

They also bought and sold sulphuric acid and used it to spray crops and weeds. (The first recorded sales of acid were in 1897).

Sulphuric acid was made by burning iron sulphide, known as pyrites, in furnaces to produce sulphur dioxide. (Later, elemental sulphur would be used). This gas in combination with oxygen and water reacted to produce the acid in large box-like structures made of special chemical lead, called lead chambers.

There were sets of lead chambers at both the old and new works and in common with the manure and tar sides of the business, were constantly being altered.

Making acid had its problems. In 1892 a leak of 25 tons of acid from the number two chamber at the old works led to one hundred tons of superphosphate being damaged.

In 1917, 'B' Glover tower collapsed, putting the set of chambers temporarily out of action.

There were often complaints from allotment holders that crops had been affected by fumes from the acid plant.

In 1926, there was an accidental escape of acid gas from a chamber that was being lifted. This led to more complaints alleging damage to allotment gardens, hedging and fruit trees.

Cecil Sands. "The old works bricklayers store was under one of the acid plant towers. Occasionally when they had a problem, acid used to run into the store and the smell was atrocious.

One of the rotten jobs was repairing brickwork in the acid plant furnaces. You lay on your back wearing breathing apparatus pointing up the brickwork. You came out looking like a Red Indian, covered in red dust. "

Leonard Smith. "After working for a year on the manure side, the foreman of the acid plants, Dan Rout, said, "Would you like to come and work on the acid plant, lad?" So I went to work as a furnaceman. The pyrites we used then was big lump ore and some of it was so large you couldn't lift it. Instead you had to roll it off the truck. With lumps of this size you tried to find the seam and then bash it with a 14lb hammer. If you were lucky the lump broke up. The rest of the lumps went into a crusher then up in an elevator to the tram road where it was hand-fed into the furnaces.

There were two types of furnaces. One was the oven type that had fire bars that protruded outside the furnace. You had a key with a big handle which was used to turn the bars to break up any clinker formed, which was then barrowed away. The other type were Herreshof furnaces which were in use at the old works."

In 1927, new Herreshof furnaces were installed at the new works acid plant to replace the oven furnaces.

Leonard Smith. "I helped to start the Herreshof furnaces up at the new works. There were three of them to start with. All the old wood that could be found on the works was used to heat up the floors of the furnaces until they were hot enough to feed the pyrites ore in.

There were seven or eight floors in each of these furnaces. A big vertical column was in the centre of each furnace which machinery turned slowly. At each floor were two 'arms' that raked the pyrites as they turned, moving it from the outside to the centre and then vice versa until it came out at the bottom as spent ore or ash.

Occasionally these 'arms' would break off and would have to be removed and a new arm inserted into the column. These 'arms' were made of cast iron in the firm's own foundry.

At first the new 'arm' was pulled up with a rope, then they installed a little electric crane which pulled the 'arm' up through a hole in the overhead floor which was made of steel mesh. One day I had a breakdown on a furnace and George Jubey, who was the day man, had been helping me to put the new 'arm' in.

"Right," said George, "that's that finished. I'm off home now." He then walked off across the mesh floor to get his coat. The next moment he had vanished from my sight; he had walked straight into the opening in the floor and had fallen to the ground below. I quickly went down the ladder and found George lying on the floor, unconscious.

There was only Jack Frost, the chamberman, and myself on shift and we had no telephone, so I got on my bike and cycled off to where one of the managers, George Brown, lived in a house opposite the office at new works. I found he was in the Conservative Club so I cycled off in that direction. I had no lights on my bike and a policeman stopped me in London Road. "Where do you think you are going," he said. When I told him he said, "I'll come with you." Eventually George Brown came back to the acid plant in his car while we followed behind on our bikes. When we got there George was still on the floor. There was an argument on how we were going to get him to hospital. "He won't go in my car," said George Brown, and he went off to phone for an ambulance.

George Jubey recovered but lost the sight in one eye as a result of the accident.

Regarding the hole in the floor. There was a steel cover plate made to fit over the hole but it took two men to lift it. The lighting at the time was also abysmal."

Two accidents on the acid plants had fatal consequences. In 1930, Mr Robert Scott, a pumpman on the acid plant at the old works, was found lying unconscious and died later in the West Norfolk and Lynn Hospital from a fractured skull. It was assumed that Mr Scott had fallen from the pump platform, which was 2'6" from the furnace level.

In 1947, an employee, Ernest Brittain, was killed by a fall of iron pyrites in the ore shed at the new works. Apparently the heap of pyrites had become hardened due to damp and was too hard for the crane grab to pick up. Mr Brittain with two others were attempting to break down the heap of pyrites using picks and shovels. They had undercut the heap by about two feet when it suddenly fell down. The fall caught Mr Brittain and covered him, resulting in multiple injuries and shock. Employees who gave evidence at the inquest and had attempted to save his life were J.M. Hawkshaw, G.W. Jubey and F.T. Wilson.

Leonard Smith. "Eventually two more Herreshof furnaces were installed, making five in all.

The columns for all five furnaces were driven by a single motor that turned a shaft in a tunnel adjacent to the furnaces. Big cogwheels on the shaft turned large chains that would have cut you in two if you had got caught up in them.

One day this woman came onto the plant. "Why haven't you got a guard on this machine," she demanded. (It turned out she was a lady factory inspector and she had come onto the plant first before going to the office). They won't put one on, I said. "They will," she said. How can you be so sure of that, I said. "I'll be back in two days," she said, "and if there isn't a guard on in that time there'll be merry hell to pay."

She was right. The carpenters were down and were soon working on guards for the chain drives.

Another awful job was loading ashes from the acid plant furnaces. In the early days, the ashes were all carried to the rail trucks in metal pans. You made a pad for your shoulder with a bag but it still made your shoulder red raw. The ash also trickled down your neck and back. When you started work the next morning the first tin that you carried was agony.

At the new works, heavy iron trams were located under the furnaces to catch the ash. When full you pulled them out on tramlines onto a turntable. Then you pushed them off into the ash shed and emptied them into a chute which went into a rail wagon. The air was thick with red dust - there was very little ventilation. There was only one closed window in the building and when I asked why it couldn't be taken out to let some air in, I got the reply 'We musn't let any of the dust get out!' The next time I was working on the crane, I knocked out the window with the crane grab. I was threatened with the sack for that!

Later the tractors came to shift the ashes. Bernard Gathercole, also known as "G" Gathercole, was the tractor driver and he was also instrumental in getting the Union in.

I was working on the night the power station chimney came down.

I had just finished charging the furnaces and walked out into the yard when I thought I saw the top of the chimney move. I lined up the chimney with the side of a building and sure enough it was moving. I went into our little hut and said, Come and have a look at this, Jack. Jack Frost had a look and said "It was designed to move." Yes, I said, but not three or four feet. We went to have our supper when suddenly everything stopped and the lights went out - the chimney had come down and broken the main cable from the power station.

I went over to the boiler house and saw the stoker, Jack Lawson. Your chimney has come down, I said. He never batted an eyelid. "Oh, has it?" he said. "I had a bit of a back draft and wondered why." You couldn't upset some of those old boys!

The chimney came down in River Shed. It was a good job it was at night because during the day the girls would have been working on the pulver and it could have killed them."

The power station chimney came down in January, 1930.

In 1927, Dr Harry Brown had investigated the possibility of supplying all the acid requirements for the works from one plant. In 1934, the acid plant at the new works was found to be in bad condition and was authorised to be replaced by a Moritz lead chamber acid plant. This plant started production in 1936 under the personal supervision of Monsieur Rene Moritz.

Leonard Smith. "Mr Eric (Mr Eric Brown) worked with me for six months. His father made him work in every department of the works. One day we were putting in a new 'arm'; they were red hot when they came out and weighed nearly 2.1/2 cwt. "Do you get any extra money for doing this?" He asked. "No, Mr Eric," I said. "You bloody well will after today," he said. "How many of these 'arms' have you put in?" I told him eight. He was as true as his word. We got 1/- for each arm put in and 8/- back pay.

I was twenty years on shift work on the acid plant. This was continuous, seven days a week - no holiday. If you took any holiday you got no pay. You finished your week of 6-2 on the Saturday and came back on at 10pm on the Sunday. This was your only day off in the month. You finished nights at 6am on the Sunday and came back at 2pm on the same day. This went on all the year round. You worked Christmas Day and Boxing Day. No extra for the Christmas Day but you received 1/- extra for working on Boxing Day."

In order for the acid to be used to make superphosphate it had first to be diluted and cooled.

Ken Nurse. "I started in 1948 on the old breaking down plant at the new works. I took acid either from the storage tanks or direct from the lead chamber plant; once per week I took the plug out of the trough at the base of the Glover tower.

The highlight to amuse visitors was to throw in a live match into a big open-topped tank in the breaking down plant. The match immediately caught fire and shot across the top of the acid like a rocket.

In those days there was no compulsory wearing of goggles and no overalls were provided. You could put on a new shirt and a pair of trousers and when they were washed they would be full of holes but you weren't aware of being splashed with acid.

You broke the acid strength down with water, cooled it and pumped it to the old and new works dens.

After the breaking down plant, I worked as a chamberman on the Moritz acid plant with Ernie Burden, Doug Gamble and Cecil Barker. The furnacemen included Ken Rout, Fred Wilson, Bill Barrett, Albert Maine, Matt Massingham, Biddy Benefer and Siddy Reynolds. George Jubey was on days, Alf Panton was the fitter and Hector Garrod the DC electrician. (The acid plant generated its own electricity from a diesel generator). Claud Russell and Bill Petchey, known as the 'old codgers', tried hard and almost succeeded in keeping the plant spotlessly clean.

There was a lift, but you never used it if there was a thunderstorm in case the power failed and you got trapped in it.

I was once up on the ammonia oxidation plant level when lightning struck the conductor on top of the tower building just above and a cloud of dust came down. I came down the stairs like a scalded cat!

When a power cut came you had to run up the outside stairs

and go into the top house over the towers and turn off the acid feeds, otherwise you could lose the plant.

When you got up there the place would be white with sulphur dioxide gas coming up from below. There was no breathing apparatus so you put a wet handkerchief over your mouth and nose, ran in and turned off one valve. You came out, took a deep breath and went in again and turned off the other valves. Finally you came out and hung over the handrail, coughing your lungs up.

Occasionally one of the seven chambers was bypassed. A hole would be cut in by the plumbers and men used to go in to dig out the sublime and put it into tubs. The protective clothing consisted of rubber boots, sack trousers and jackets. It was a filthy job but it was on bonus."

The author. "I spent some time in the Moritz acid plant in 1950 doing the lab tests. On my first visit I was introduced to the plant manager, Mr J.M. Hawkshaw, who issued words of warning. "If something drips on your head," he said, don't look up because the next drip will be in your eye. If you see a puddle of rainwater, don't walk in it because it could be acid.

In those days, lab staff were issued with khaki coats. Mine was still looking quite respectable until someone knocked over a sample pot of hot sulphuric acid that was standing on the lab bench in the acid plant. The contents poured down the front of my coat and in the few seconds it took me to take it off, the parts of the coat contaminated with acid had turned from khaki to a shade of green! After being washed, the front completely disintegrated and hung down in strips.

The laboratory of the acid plant was on the first floor and the single bench was covered in sheet lead. The sink tap was kept running continuously.

The sample pots were works of art made by the leadburners. You took one up to the next floor in the lift and left the gate open. At this level was the base of the Glover tower. The acid made in the lead chambers was concentrated in this tower and had to be tested regularly. The acid left the tower by an open-topped trough, spitting and giving off choking fumes that also made your face sting. My routine was to dip the lead pot into this steaming trough at the same time shutting my eyes to avoid any splashes. I then retraced my steps to the lift as quickly as possible, consistent with not spilling any of the acid.

Back in the lab my first action after putting down the pot of acid, was to get my hand under the running tap. Another unpleasant place was the ground floor pumphouse. Here, powerful pumps mounted on plinths pumped up acid and acid containing nitre, known as nitrous vitriol, from open-topped tanks to the tops of the Glover and Gay Lussac towers eighty to ninety feet above the pumphouse. Occasionally one of the lead pipes on the pressure side of one of the pumps would burst and a spray of acid would be ejected all over the pumphouse. The pump motor control switches were mounted on a wall opposite the battery of pumps which meant that someone would have to run the gauntlet of the acid spray to reach the relevant switch. That someone was the chamberman who would put a sack over his head and make a dash for it.

There was always a standby pump (the acid plant was designed to run continuously) so the chamberman would change over to this and arrange for the leadburners to repair the burst pipe."

The leadburners' workshop was alongside the Nar Valley drain at the new works and sample pots, lead floats (used in acid storage tanks) and various other lead artifacts hung from hooks above the benches. There were also facilities to melt small amounts of lead which would then be ladled into a fluted mould to make the lead solder strips used when welding sheet lead.

In earlier days the leadburners' shop was at the old works.

Reg Rout. "In 1934, at the age of 14, I started with the leadburners at the old works for 7/6d per week. The workshop was near the acid plant. Tom Arrowsmith, the father of Matt Arrowsmith, was in charge. I helped with patching lead on the acid plant lead chambers and repairing lead pipes, etc. I used to go in on a Sunday for 2/- to wash out the Gay Lussac tower."

On January 31st, 1953, the waters of the great flood came to the Moritz plant and put out the five Herreshof furnaces for good. It was also the end for the lead chamber plant. A decision was made not to try and restart the plant and all the acid was then made on the new plant which was parallel to the old chamber plant and produced sulphuric acid by the contact process.

Eric Broad. "After the great flood, I had the job with men from the new works granulation plant that was shut down, of dismantling the old Moritz lead chamber plant. There was a tall windbreaking wall on the westward side of the chamber plant that went up to the full height of the box chambers, a distance of some eighty to ninety feet. Legend had it that five gold sovereigns had been buried in the wall at the topping out ceremony way back in the 1930's. The wall was pulled down carefully, brick by brick, but no trace of the sovereigns was ever found!

The Moritz lead chamber plant, September 1951. The foundations for the contact acid plant under construction.

courtesy of R Goodchild

Apart from being a different process, the contact acid plant produced acid of about 98% strength as compared with the strongest acid made on the chamber plant which was around 78%.

One drop of 98% sulphuric acid on the skin produced an immediate burn irrespective of how fast you treated it with water. Old domestic baths full of water were located at strategic points and anyone unlucky enough to get splashed with acid was literally thrown in.

B(Joe)Bennett. "I was with Alfie Panton repacking an acid pump. It was a freezing cold day with white frost everywhere. Suddenly some acid came out of the pump gland and splashed Alfie in the face. The next moment he was shouting that he had acid in his eyes. I got hold of him and pushed him into the bath - there was a layer of ice on the surface of the water. Another fitter who was there said, "You rotten devil, you did that deliberately." But it saved his eyesight. He came and thanked me afterwards for what I had done."

Ken Nurse. "I went to work on the contact acid plant when it first started and was working in the washing section breaking down strong acid; it used to boil when broken down with water.

There was an open-topped measuring box and the acid flowed through a vertical line of holes and you counted these to give an estimate on how much acid was flowing. Suddenly there was a blow-back and acid flowed over me (I believe it was due to an airlock in the pipe downstream). I had a hat and goggles on and the acid didn't go in my eyes but ran down my back and behind one of my ears. I got in a water trough and lay down in the water. Somebody directed a hose charged with water at me and I remember thinking, if I don't get up for some air soon I'm going to drown.

Dr Dean was called in and treated my burns which took a long time to heal up."

Chapter 9

SUPPLIES AND DISPATCH

The location of the works alongside the River Nar and with easy access to the railway network meant that the company could obtain its raw materials and despatch products by rail, road or water.

They were always on the lookout for ways of reducing transport costs. For example, in 1889, they imported sulphate of ammonia into the works via Boston at 9/6d per ton because a Lynn shipping company was asking 10/- per ton freight.

Horses and carts were the first means of transport used on the roads. The company employed horsemen and had a stable block; in 1893 it is recorded that the old stables were pulled down and a new one built in its place. An old accounts ledger records the purchase of 'carrots for horse' - £1.10.0d.

In the period between 1897 and 1898, they negotiated with the Great Eastern Railway and the Midland and Great Northern Railway to connect their sidings to the respective rail systems. A connection to a siding at the old works and to the new works was made by the G.E.R. from the harbour branch railway line. A connection into the new works was made by the M & G N Railway, from South Lynn.

In 1904 WNF hired four railway wagons. It is believed these were used mainly for bringing in bulk coal for both the retail market and their own use. In 1901, they purchased over 4,000 tons of coal, mainly from Ellis and Everard. The company continued buying and selling coal up to and including the second world war. Customers could select from a variety of coals including Sherwood best hards, Newstead slack,, Natwall hards and smalls and Smithy nuts.

Sidney Oakes. "I started on the works as a labourer in 1933. The fixed wages were £1.4.8d per week, 7am-5pm and Saturday morning. Part of the job was unloading coal and 3 men could empty a 12 ton coal truck in 20 minutes."

Reg Rout. "The coal was kept in several open storage bays in the old works yard. It was delivered around Lynn by Tom Soden driving a small four wheeled tractor called the 'Imp' which pulled a trailer."

The yard at the old works, 1933. The rail line crossing gates on the Wisbech Road are in the background.

courtesy of R Barham

Reg Rout. "After serving as a stoker in the Royal Navy in the second world war, I came back in 1946 to work as a stoker on the old works granulation plant. The furnace burnt small coal and a gang of us used to come in on a Saturday morning to offload a coal wagon with shovels for 2/6d each."

Extensive use was made of the River Nar and its connections into the waterway systems of the Fens for delivering fertiliser to farms.

In 1874 the Company were employing an engine driver, a Mr Smith, who worked a 58.1/2 hour week for £1.4.4d, therefore it may be assumed that they had a railway engine. It is recorded that they purchased a new locomotive (No. 632) from Peckett and Sons of Bristol in 1912.

Les Figgis. "In the old days at the new works, trucks loaded with phosphate rock or pyrites were pushed up an incline between the floors by a steam locomotive. To get up the incline the engine had to get up a head of steam. I was working overhead in the baghouse at the time and used to get smoked out with the mixture of steam and smoke.

When they were offloading phosphate, a man had to lay down and trip the trapdoor under the bottom of each truck so that the contents would fall down onto the floor below.

If they were offloading pyrites for the acid plant, the trucks would be pushed on a bit further. When a truck was in position, the doors were dropped on both sides and the pyrites offloaded by men with shovels."

In 1932, a secondhand truck tippler was purchased for offloading raw materials from rail wagons. The LNER (London and North Eastern Railway) agreed to the use of this equipment in 1936 and it was used for the first time to deal with 3100 tons of Constantine phosphate in bulk from Bona in North Africa. The phosphate was offloaded at Boal Quay from the vessel Ingertoft, which was turned-round in two days on 29th and 30th November, 1936.

The truck tippler was damaged when a line of trucks was accidentally shunted into it the following year, but despite this set back proved successful. In 1951, three new truck tipplers were installed during the big expansion programme so that all bulk raw materials could be discharged by this method.

Les Figgis. "From the baghouse I went to the truck tippler operation. There were three truck tipplers that used to swing the whole truck, loaded with bulk material, upside down by a counterbalanced operation. I was in charge of the pyrites tippler, George Griggs the phosphate tippler and Charley Wiffen, the potash tippler.

I next started work as a shunter on the rail operation and when one of the drivers, Lenny Pidgeon, left, I took his job. The other loco drivers were Eric Plowright, Eric Raspberry and Jim Bunn. We worked shifts during the season to keep the Nar shed loaders supplied with box wagons. We used to work the loco up to a plate on a rail sleeper near the harbour branch line which said 'B.R.(E) Maintenance ends here.' There were eight rail bays at the Nar shed and a big siding. We used to pull twenty four box wagons there to service the operation.

I drove 'Dr Harry', and the other diesel loco was 'Patricia.' When we were on shift I drove 'Dr Harry' one week and 'Patricia' the next."

The pyrites truck tippler, later used to offload bulk sulphur.

courtesy of R Goodchild

It was traditional for barges, tugboats and railway engines to be named after members of the Brown family. Thus Dr Harry (purchased in 1945) was named after Dr H.C. Brown. 'Peter', (the steam locomotive) after the son of Mr Eric Brown and 'Patricia' after a daughter. This was the last loco purchased by the Company, who took delivery of the 80 BHP 0/4/0 diesel in December 1950.

Les Figgis at the controls of 'Patricia'. Shunter, 'Horry' Marsters is on the right.

courtesy of Les Figgis

The method of dispatching product changed very little over the years and, before the advent of pallets and the fork lift truck, depended on the labour and skill of men to load barges, rail wagons, farm carts and lorries. The short three month season meant a dawn to dusk operation with a queue of lorries waiting to be loaded.

W.G. Gemmell. "In February and March, lorries were clogging up the site and continually causing an obstruction in Saddlebow Road. The police often complained about the queue of lorries. Early delivery rebates were used as an incentive for farmers to buy and stock early, thus getting rid of the mad Spring rush."

Up till 1937, all fertiliser was dispatched in 16 stone bags, but at this time the Company started to introduce 12 stone bags for farmers who wanted this smaller size.

Special, valved paper sacks were introduced at the end of the second world war and held one cwt of granular fertiliser. It was now possible to bag and store this material for future delivery.

W.G. Gemmell. "China' Clark, one of the loaders, was most upset when the 1cwt bag came in. "Do you realise I've got to walk twice as far now?" he said."

The stacks built by the loaders were works of art.

Mancell Ryan. "You could put a spirit level on the sides of any stack they built, they were that straight."

Building a stack. 'Agga' Beales and Sidney Oakes are on the stack. Alf Lammiman is putting bags on the portable conveyor.
courtesy of R Goodchild

A gang of five men would be involved in breaking the stack down and loading from it. The stack would have been built up in steps and two men would start at the top pulling down bags. They would time this operation so that the bags rolled down the stack to arrive in the right positions for two men running away with sack barrows. They fed a slatted, inclined conveyor which supplied the bags to the loader.

The quantities loaded were prodigious. On 2nd March 1938, a record was established when 1,750 tons of fertiliser were dispatched from the various floors. It is not known whether this record was ever beaten.

Sidney Oakes. "The greatest weight of sacks I ever moved was 256.1/2 tons in one day between 7am and 5.15pm."

The loaders included Sidney Oakes, Herbert Mace, Walter Nicholls, G.W. 'Gummy' Reeve, Joe Mitchell, 'China' Clark, Peter Clark, John Gamble, 'Yoggy' Gamble, Fred Funnell, Bill Fawkes, 'Agga' Beales, Fred Howlett and 'Dubby' Jordan.

Mancell Ryan. "I worked for a time in the Nar shed. They had started to use plastic sacks. 'Nod' Nicholls was bagging up and I was running the full 1cwt plastic sacks through the heat sealer. I then went with the loaders and when I first started I had trouble getting them into the right position. 'China' Clark said to me, "How many times do you get paid to touch a bag?" Once, I said. "Then," said 'China,' "Only touch it once.""

Bill Fawkes. "When the bag came down you caught it across the back of your shoulders and neck. You took one pace forward, dropped your shoulder and slammed it down into the exact spot with your arm guiding it. When you were learning how to do it you took two or even three steps forward. The secret was to take one step and drop your shoulder."

WNF also had their own transport and several drivers would be engaged delivering direct to farmers.

Bert Dye. "I went on to driving lorries and took over an old 6 wheel rigid lorry from Horry Catton, carting all over the place in Lincolnshire and Norfolk, taking fertiliser to farmers. In those days it was 16 stone hessian bags and very often you had to offload on your own. Then the new Bedford lorries came in and driving those were Albert Fish, Jimmy Stewart and Lenny Catton. I went on to drive an articulated Atkinson diesel which had three bodies, bulk, flat bottom and a tanker."

Other drivers included Fred Stokes, Tony White, Tom Barrett, Albert Ellis, Percy Ellis, Ivan Fincham, Narny Catton, George Moyse and Alf Needham.

Alf Needham. "I finished on the Atkinson diesel tanker and ran shifts with Fred Stokes transporting ammonia from Flixborough to the WNF store. They also had three or four long-nosed Albion tankers that they used to bring in sulphuric acid during the early 1950's when there was an acid shortage."

One of the loading stages at River shed, 1933.
courtesy of R Barham

Chapter 10

THE OFFICE STAFF

In 1889 a contract was agreed for a new office and laboratory to be built at the north-east end of the Company's property fronting the Wisbech Road, on the west side of the River Nar. The laboratory was in the upper part of the building.

Derek Foreman. "I joined in the office on 1.1.1930 aged 14, still in short trousers, as a junior clerk in the order and dispatch department where I worked with Bill Harris. Bert Barron was the department head. The office started at 9am and we often worked on Saturday and Sunday during the season, doing consignment notes.

There was a strict 'no smoking' rule in the office. You nipped in the toilet if you wanted a smoke. Joe Brown, the son of James Brown, and Bill Baxter, were the accountants. Edith Brown, sister of Joe, also worked upstairs in the office.

In 1930 everything sold was powder fertiliser in hessian sacks. Local farmers used to collect their fertiliser by horse and cart. We used to get a call from J.H. Dennick to say so many carts were coming up for fertiliser.

We also dealt with rabbit skins, (horrible smell) hoof and horn meal, dried blood, and bone meal. There were no typewriters, and work was done with a pen dipped in ink. B.M. Targett, used to do very good handwriting and made out all the invoices by hand. Our office did the pricing and the figures were then sent up to Mr Targett.

In addition to Boal Quay Wharfingers which was run from the office, the Company had a warehouse in Bridge Street, Lynn, next to the Hulk Inn called 'Springalls'."

Mrs W.N.Nurse. "My uncle was a Percy Thorne who died in 1929 aged 39. He paid the wages and operated the starting and finishing buzzer. He used to take me into the office on a Sunday and taught me how to use the telephone. I remember it had a long vertical stem and you spoke into a fixed mouthpiece."

At first only one lady had worked in the office and that was Edith Brown. Then in 1931, two ladies started, Mary Hampson and Madge Mussett. Mary Hampson was engaged by Mr A.C.K. Sheppard, known as 'stilts' because of his height, who was secretary to Dr Harry Brown. She began work as a telephonist, learned shorthand and typing and gradually moved up to become secretary to Mr D.H. Reid, the company secretary and general manager.

Mary Hampson.
courtesy D Foreman

When Dr Harry was dictating to his secretary, a red lamp would come on outside his office. This had quite an effect on his wife when she first saw it - much to the amusement of the staff.

Madge Otterspoor. "I started work in the accounts office with Joe Brown and Bill Baxter at the age of 16, in 1936. A man called Martin Luther worked in a side office to the office block; it had a door opening out to the side where the men clocked on and off. He told me there was a vacancy in the accounts department. Before I could put in an application Joe Brown came to see me.

Dr Harry Brown was in charge. He was a cross patch and didn't speak to anyone. He had a thing about men and women working together. He may not have been a well person. A lift was installed in about 1936 so he may have had difficulty in climbing stairs. (His office was on the first floor at the head of the stairway).

Because of the 'no smoking' rule in the office, Stanley Elms used to smoke in front of a coal fire and puff the smoke up the chimney, in case Dr Harry came in.

Times were very good in the office. The cleaners lit a coal fire in the winter. A bonus was paid in the June which was useful for holidays. It was about £15; a lot of money in those days. (Later the bonus stopped). The Company also paid National Insurance for staff.

There were six girls in the office, including myself. Two of them worked in the Boal Quay office; Mr Sheppard was in charge of Boal Quay. Staff numbered about twenty in total. I remember that Mr B.M. Targett also did the share certificates in wonderful copperplate handwriting. J.G. Newby was one of the auditors and came to work as an accountant in succession to Joe Brown.

In 1936 all the ledgers were hand written. J.G. Newby introduced accounting machines and I went on a 14 day course to Remington-Rand in London. During the war the staff were told that the gas works bridge was mined. I don't know where the story came from, but we used to look at the bridge and wonder whether it would go up one day! The Company sold coal and anthracite during the war.

After the war there was a succession of people coming and going in the office. The staff mushroomed and two Nissen huts, fixed together in parallel as one unit, appeared. I believe they came from an RAF Station, having previously served as a Chapel. After the first few years there appeared to be little maintenance done with the result that the roof became thin and the walls dirty. It was extremely cold in winter because there was no insulation and the heat went straight out. They kept putting off repairs. We were told there was going to be a new building, in fact we were in there for 18 years. In 1963, a particularly cold winter, the heating broke down and I worked in sweater, cardigan, coat and boots. At around this time the firm brought in a time and motion study team. (One member of staff was made redundant as a result). The rain used to come in through the roof and I put up an umbrella to keep the water off an accounting machine which was on hire. I remember that this time and motion study man came in to the office and his face was a picture when he saw the umbrella!

The floor was made of concrete with metal walls and roof and when the accounting machines were on the noise was deafening. Mrs Williamson or Mrs Bone used to come round with the tea trolley and tell us that we appeared to be the only office that was really working!"

W.G. Gemmell. "I started in January 1949 in the sales office with Derek Foreman, Cliff Human and Billy Hammond. Billy Hodd did the tickets, Stanley Elms was on the road and Len Elms was in charge. In 1952 I moved into outside sales with Stanley Elms and Bill Flintham from Boston.

The majority of sales were through markets and I attended Lynn on Tuesday at the Corn Hall, Bury St. Edmunds on Wednesday, Fakenham on Thursday, Dereham or Diss on Friday and Norwich on Saturday. Monday was office work day. Bill Flintham used to do Boston and Ely Markets.

Up till about April, 1950, petrol was till rationed but there was enough petrol allocation to get to markets. Initially I travelled on a 1937 Velocette 350cc motor bike to Fakenham market.

Edgar Broad used to do certain markets during the war. He went to Norwich market every Saturday. Mr Reid and Mr Libbey used to attend Lynn Market occasionally to maintain contact with farmers.

When granulated fertiliser came in, farmers were only allowed to take a certain percentage of their requirements in granular form because the new plant at the old works was only producing about 120 tons a day. Merchants were allowed to take 10% of their total requirement as granular fertiliser. We kept a list of all special compounds in a so-called 'marks' book. Many of the farmers had their own special mixings. The coming of granulated product put an end to this because it was no longer economical to keep stopping and changing mixings.

Soil analysis was free. When powders were made, we made special mixings to suit soil conditions. You can't do this with granular.

In the days before computers, Edgar Broad used to check what orders were in, write these on the back of a scrap of paper and then go and check the stocks. He met with the foremen at the same time every day."

The normal starting point for new entrants straight from school was the position of office boy. Many of the people who held senior positions in the Company started this way and gradually worked their way up. They included C.W.K. Stokes and Edgar Broad. The latter began in 1904 it is believed addressing envelopes for 5/-per week. He went to night school, became an accountant and eventually was appointed works manager. He retired in 1958 after 54 years service. The last office boy to be appointed was Chris Boxall.

Chris Boxall. "I was employed as office boy by Bob Pinnock at a weekly wage of £4 before deductions, joining at 16 in 1962 and leaving in 1965. I was promised a six month spell after which I would then go into one of the offices on Wisbech Road. I was actually employed as an office boy for 13 months before becoming a junior sales clerk.

Trained by the outgoing office boy, Eric, (who went into production records with Elwyn Bush), I was put in the charge of the commissionaire Bob Winterbone and his young blonde helper, Sandra Roome. My main job was to deliver the mail round the office and the factory and to act as courier between the National Dock Labour Board, Garland and Flexman and Boal Quay, etc.

Internal main was delivered and picked up from the various offices by means of a large green postal book. Everything else was done by means of a rather dilapidated old trade bike. Twice a day I would ride from the offices and Nissen huts on Wisbech Road to the offices on Saddlebow Road, calling at Black Shed, the safety hut, the stores and the garage along the way. The office mail was also delivered on a twice daily basis and I also made a twice daily visit into town. The rest of my day was spent in general front office duties, opening post, etc, and welcoming visitors.

Riding that old trade bike was something of a chore and it wasn't long before the thing seized up on me. That was when Bill Pearman and his garage boys stepped in to help. They took the bike away and completely rebuilt it, giving it a fresh coat of paint and a brand new straw basket. The trade plate beneath the cross bar was painted WNF in large white letters. Life became a great deal easier after this refurbishment.

Life on the trade bike was not without its hazards. I recall crossing the railway lines on one occasion when the front wheel of the bike got caught in the gap between the lines and the wooden crossing sleepers. I came off, badly grazing my knee, but I was more concerned with rescuing the bike from the path of an oncoming train which was shunting wagons of phosphate from Boal Quay into the works. I managed to pull the bike free in the nick of time

My daily trips into town always took longer than they should have done because I was always running errands for practically everyone in the office. The secretaries would want shoes taken to the menders or various items purchased. Every Friday evening it was my job to get 100 cigarettes for a senior member of staff to last him over the weekend. Another special job was going for the Christmas sandwiches on Board day meetings. These were specially prepared at the Globe Hotel and carried back in due solemnity in the pannier of the trade bike!"

Chapter 11

THE ENGINEERS

The Company could boast that if something broke they had someone, either to repair it or make a new one. If they needed a new building, they had people with building skills and as new plants were introduced many were made in their own workshops.

Maintenance was also a big cost item. Wear and tear and the corrosive effect of some of the raw materials meant a continuous programme of repair and replacement was necessary.

The range of craftsmen available was impressive and included electricians, fitters, specialised machinists, platers, welders, blacksmiths, carpenters, joiners, a pattern maker, a cooper, plumbers, lead burners, foundry workers, bricklayers, scaffolders, painters, a rigger, an instrument mechanic, a beltman, garage mechanics, a tool and tackle storekeeper and draughtsmen. They also took on engineering apprentices.

Many items were made in the foundry which was alongside the Nar Valley drain, but before it could be cast, a wooden pattern would be made by the pattern maker. This would be the exact size and shape of the required component. The pattern would then be pressed firmly down into a metal casting box full of special sand. This would make a mould into which molten metal would be poured. When cold the casting would be removed. The new component would then have to be machined in the workshop.

As engineering requirements grew, a much larger workshop was installed in 1930 alongside the River Nar on the freshwater side of the penstock.

Tom Snape. "The workshop had one motor which powered a long overhead shaft. Everything was run from this by way of belts and pulleys. To stop a machine you used 'striking gear.' This looked like a fork with two prongs and you used this to move the driving belt from the fast pulley to a loose pulley which just idled around without driving the machine.

I came back after the war and learnt plating with Walter Bedwell. I also went on an electric welding course. The other people in the platers' gang, while I was there, were Walter Bedwell, Gordon Bedwell, Jack Mawby, Alfie Lane, Dick Eglen, Ted Twite, Ron

Whiley, Bill Dack, Tom Denny, Noel Parr, Arthur Mitchell, Bert Wain, Jack Adcock, Dave Baugh, Jim McKenna, Mick McKenna and Henry Bunting. When Walter Bedwell left I took over the platers' shop.

In addition to machines and the platers' shop, the main workshop contained two forges and a carpenters' shop."

The main workshop circa 1950.

Foreground, L to R: Sid Howard, Mick McKenna, Tom Snape, Walter Watson and Dave Jary. Middle Distance: Dick Castle and Duncan Colquhoun.

courtesy of R Goodchild

The workshop was equipped with an overhead electric travelling crane. Later the forges were removed from the workshop and one of them was relocated in a new building at the north end of the workshop. The carpenters' shop was also removed to a new building on the west side of the workshop.

Tom Snape. "The turner was Bill Day and before him were Fred Petts and George Clitheroe. The drillers were Derek Ellis and Walter Watson. George Skipper operated the shaping machine. Included with the carpenters and joiners were Wilf Barnaby, the foreman, Wilf Kirk, Bob Harris, Andy Mayer, Billy Ketteringham, George Watson, Bert Targett, the pattern maker, Jack Thurlow, Alf Latus, Fred Taylor, and Ron Edgeley (his father George used to drive 'Peter', the steam loco).

The workshop was as dark as a railway tunnel, especially in the winter months when it was difficult to read the chalk marks on the metal."

Bert Dye. "In 1947 I started as a temporary worker with Len Joplin, 'Bubbles' Crowther and Doug Coston, working on 'A' floor bagging up compound and sewing up sacks. In April, after the season had finished I was offered a job in the workshop as a blacksmith's striker. I decided to give it a go. I worked with blacksmith Fred Gant, the other was Duncan Colquhoun, who had Dick Castle as striker.

Washing facilities were a bit primitive but we did have hot water. We used to heat up a piece of iron rod and when it was red hot, plunge it into a bucket of cold water. Men then queued up to wash their hands in the bucket and then dried them on a sack hung on a nail."

Jack Adcock. "I came from Dodmans as a plater/welder in 1949 and started in Walter Bedwell's gang. The German machines (Lanvermeyers) were still running and one of my jobs was to repair the one in Black Shed at the old works.

I remember one job when I nearly came to grief. I was working up near the crane track in the Nar Shed looking for loose rivets. When you found one you removed it and installed a high tensile bolt. I was leaning over the track, ring spanner in one hand, when one end of the spanner touched the trolley wires along the side of the shed. There were three strands of copper wire that supplied power to the cranes. Unbeknown to me, someone had just switched on the power. There was a flash and I got a shock; fortunately it wasn't serious which I put down to the fact that I was wearing rubber boots.

We were always playing practical jokes. One of the carpenters, Jack Thurlow, used to collect the eggs every day from Mr Reid's chickens, put them under his cap, then take them up to the office. One day I patted him on the head knowing he had eggs under his cap. I kept out of his way for several days after that.

One of the painters was nearly bald and very self-conscious about this. He always wore a hat. He used to come into work wearing a cap, go over to where he kept his old trilby and quickly change over hats. One day, one of the carpenters put a 3" nail through his trilby and when he went to take it down naturally it didn't come!"

Cecil Sands. "I went into the bricklaying gang with Bob Raven in 1928. . My first week's pay was 15/- This went up to 35/8d with overtime.

I helped to build the new laboratory next to the office on Wisbech Road. I also did brickwork in Kerkham's warehouse, the gable ends at New Shed and built the breaking down plant at new works. Another job was the 'spotters 'hut' which was used by men on firewatch duties during the second world war. The painters' shop was underneath this.

Towards the end of the war, I remember being on a scaffold working on the chimney of No.2 Wisbech Road (this house belonged to the Company at the time), which is a very tall house, when an aircraft came over so low that the sudden gust of wind nearly took me off the stack. I didn't have time to see whether it was one of ours!"

Eddy Betts. "I worked for a time as an electrician's mate with Les Norris, looking after the battery operated trams that worked on the floors. The batteries had to be put on charge every night ready for the next day. The charging shed for the batteries was next to the power station at the new works. Charley Peacock was in charge of the generating house where DC current was generated. The generators were steam powered and there were two boilers, both of which were fed with coal by shovel. The shift firemen at that time were George Holmes, Alf Curtis and Arthur Hickman.

After the season had finished, I used to go into the boilers in the summertime, chipping the insides with a compressed air operated jack hammer. The noise was deafening and I had to wear ear plugs. I got 1/-a day 'black money' for doing this."

In 1938 the price per unit for electricity had fallen to where it was now economical for the Company to buy rather than generate electricity for themselves. As a consequence, they shut down the generating plant. However, they kept it on standby in case economic conditions should alter.

Stan Hemeter. "I started after the main electrical installation had been completed in about 1951. There were several of us electricians started by P Starkings who was the electrical engineer at the time. Peter Graver was in charge of the electricians and Sid Woodhouse his deputy. Included amongst the electricians were Bob Sheard, Bob Finney, Reg (the Duke) Dinnage, Hector Garrod, Graham (Willy) Dewart, Lenny Cook, George Mayes, Peter Knowles (Instrument mechanic), Fred Marchant, Derek (Dike) Shears, George (Dacka) Johnson, Derek Allen, Les Barron, Pat Walden, Pat Hall, Fred Chilvers, David (Seagull) Childs, Clifford (TCP) Jones, Stan Marriott, Joe Groom, Peter Griffiths, and Gordon (Aggy) Ellis. The electricians' shop was alongside the main stores.

An institution was the 'heavy gang', who had a hut with a corrugated iron roof alongside the coal dump, about halfway between the old and the new works. There were no cranes. If there was something heavy that needed shifting, they moved it, including putting back rail wagons that had become derailed. Some of the gang were 'Ossie' Horsely, Percy Pottle and Stan Plumley. (Earlier George Fisher had been in charge of this gang which included 'Nissens' Beckett)."

Ken Thompson. "I joined the electricians late in 1953. Originally electric power at WNF was DC and all motors operated on this current. The mills at the old and new works each used a 1000 horse power DC motor that drove everything by belts and shafting. All DC motors had brush gear. Eventually the site went on to AC motors and each piece of equipment had its own motor. The Company used mainly LSE motors (Laurence, Scott & Electromotors Ltd) and Allen West switchgear. This became quite advanced with sequencing gear installed. This meant that if one part stopped, the items downstream stopped automatically. Switchgear that could be isolated was also installed so that belt conveyors could be isolated for maintenance. The system was to have a duplicate motor for every single motor in use so if one broke down it could be quickly and easily replaced. The former power station at the new works was used as a motor store."

Stan Hemeter. "After P Starkings left, Stan Waterworth became chief engineer with Charles Richman his deputy. The mechanical foremen were Bob Roberts and Dave Jary, under Reg Brown. Cliff Bussens was the machine shop foreman and I remember his skill. He sharpened a drill bit for me one day when I was working in the workshop and it went through a steel beam like butter.

There were several characters. Amongst these was Alf Curston, one of the watchmen who looked after the south end of the site that included the workshop and the sports pavilion. I asked him if he was nervous going down there in the dark and he told me that he had a six foot tall Indian spirit guide who used to walk with him."

John Batch. "I started straight from King Edward VII Grammar School at 17 in 1944. Starting pay was 25/- per week as a draughtsman. After National Service I returned in 1948 as a draughtsman/trainee engineer at £3.0.0 per week. After getting City and Guilds ONC, which was as far as the Lynn Technical College went, I made plans to leave so that I could carry on further study. Mr Eric Brown got to hear about this and made arrangements for me to attend Norwich Tech. on a day off per week. I believe I was the first person to get day release for study. One of my first jobs was drawing plans of knives for the Lanvermeyer bagging machine.

Certain unpleasant jobs were done at a premium rate above the normal rate for the job. Sometimes when there was a breakdown the rate for the job had to be negotiated. Rates agreed were usually around 1/2d or 1d per hour - 2d per hour would be for a really terrible job. If the same job came up again the men might say, "We're not going in for that money!" At that point the rate had to be re-negotiated. Everytime you agreed a new rate you set a precedent.

The toilets for the workshop were on the river bank and they had a trough of water, fed from the river, underneath. The men used to play tricks on new apprentices, like lighting a piece of paper and letting it float down on the water when they were siting on the toilet!

In about 1955 a development department was started and I moved to 9, Nelson Street as chief draughtsman and designer. The drawing office was relocated in one of the two houses on Wisbech Road opposite the main office block. H.C. Kidd was in charge at Nelson Street with P Curry, development engineer, John Hill, mechanical engineer and David Little, a chemical engineer.

Later I became an assistant engineer with W.C. Richman, reporting to the chief engineer Stan Waterworth. I was in charge of maintenance on the acid plants and Charles Richman in charge of maintenance on the fertiliser section."

One of the key figures in the maintenance department was Reg Brown.

Jack Adcock. "I thought he was one of the finest engineers around. If it was repairable, he could repair it."

The author. "Reg Brown, who lived close to the works, used to come back every evening preceded by his black labrador, to have a look round and check the progress of any maintenance work. If a breakdown occurred that was too big for the duty shift fitters to handle he would be called out.

Calling out Reg in the early hours wasn't lightly contemplated because he was known for a fierce response if his sleep was disturbed! On one occasion the watchmen were reluctant to go and wake him up, so I went. I knocked at the door and Reg opened it. It was evident that I had aroused him from sleep. "What do you want?" Reg, the granulator main shaft has sheared in two, I replied. "Well what the ——— do you expect me to do about it? (Pause) Alright, I'll be there in a minute". And he was. After a quick inspection, a gang of platers were called out. They worked all night and by 9am the plant was ready to restart. That was the calibre of Reg Brown and the tradesmen who worked for him."

Chapter 12

THE LABORATORY

From the beginning the Company had given a high priority to producing quality products, initially sending samples to Dr Voelcker and Professor Sibson for analyses.

Where the first laboratory was located is not known, but new offices were built at the old works fronting the Wisbech Road with a laboratory on the top floor, where it remained until 1930, when a new large laboratory was built alongside the office block.

Amongst the early chemists were C.E. Truffitt, who became head chemist and resigned in 1929 after 32 years service, Bill Cox, Eddy Adcock, Graham English and Les Brooks.

Dr Harry Brown, himself a chemist and a Fellow of the Institute of Chemists, had expressed a wish in the Company's annual circular of 1934 that "the customers should look upon the works together with our laboratory as part of their farm organisation."

The laboratory staff not only tested raw materials and products, they sampled gases leaving the chimneys of the acid plants and dens, to ensure pollution laws were not broken. They also tested soils. Gradually this important aspect of the analysis programme became free and a complete advisory service also became available. As an expansion of this service Richard P. Libbey B.Sc., a botanist, was appointed as an agricultural advisor.

John Williamson. "I started in the main laboratory in 1947. The lab personnel consisted of Lance Leech, Bill Cox, Eddy Adcock, Lionel(Frisky)Francis and Graham English. Les Brooks was in charge. Everyone wore khaki lab coats. You made your own wash bottles and your glass cloth was made from a sugar sack - nothing was wasted.

For the first three months I worked on phosphate determinations and did the washing up. You worked with an analyst and had to agree within .01% of his results before you were allowed to undertake analysis yourself. I then graduated on to nitrogens which I did for six months. Eventually you were allowed to do potash determinations; this could take as long as two years. You were never allowed to do raw material analysis. Occasionally we were allowed to do ash samples which meant grinding the sample down with an iron pestle and mortar, wearing a hole in your hand in the process! You then burnt off the residual sulphur in a nickel crucible. In the shift lab, later on, we had a hammer mill to do the hard work but this took a lot of cleaning out afterwards.

We used to weigh up all samples at one go. In the balance room you started on balances that used individual weights, including tiny platinum weights that you handled with a pair of tweezers. You gradually worked your way up the seniority scale which entitled you to use balances of a more advanced type.

One day we had eighteen or nineteen sets of solids made up in solution in flasks. They were all lined up on the island bench ready to be put in the shaker when somebody came past and accidentally knocked one over with a result that they all went down like a line of dominoes.

Occasionally a sample of river water was brought in for analysis. Les Brooks used to test this by dipping a finger in the sample and tasting it!

In addition to doing the washing up, the junior had to get the coffee and tea rations from the canteen and get the washing soap from the stores. Soap was on ration, so you had to get a requisition signed by Les Brooks and countersigned by Reg Brown. You had to get in early otherwise it would all go, so I used to go to Reg on the first day of the month and he would always say, "You're bloody early, aren't you?"

Everyone in the lab had their little foibles. Bill Cox's routine when he first came in was to look at the paper then take out a cigarette and light it. After taking a couple of puffs he would nip it out. That cigarette lasted till lunchtime. The same rigmarole would be repeated in the afternoon. Eddy Adcock smoked a pipe. He used to light his pipe with a match and then the bunsen burner. The spent match would then be placed on a big stack of spent matches on his bench. He would then use the dead matches to light his pipe via the bunsen."

The main laboratory, circa 1950/1951.

Clockwise:- Geoff Wilkinson, Colin Stevens, Lance Leech, Eddy Adcock, John Allflatt, Les Brooks, Peter Morley and Bill Cox.

courtesy of R Goodchild

With the expansion programme of the post war period well underway, it became necessary to have a small laboratory on the works to support the new plants by carrying out round-the-clock tests. This shift lab opened in mid 1951 and was situated in one end of a former nissen hut alongside the Saddlebow Road at the new works. The rest of the hut consisted of foremens' offices. The original four that manned this lab were Colin Stevens, John Williamson, Peter Morley and the author.

In 1952, a break with tradition occurred when Joyce Colquhoun began work as an analyst in the previously male-dominated main laboratory.

Back in the shift lab, as the work load expanded so did the personnel. There were now two people on duty per shift and John Williamson was in charge on days. Instrumentation was also becoming available.

John Williamson. "Gordon Nelson, the chief chemist by this time, had introduced peristaltic pumps. These were wheels with bars that rotated progressively causing liquid to be pumped along a plastic tube. This was the nearest approach to automatic analyses and I believe that WNF was one of the first in the fertiliser industry to adopt this method."

The original shift laboratory remained in use for ten years until a new office and welfare block was built in 1961 and a lab was installed on the first floor.

Chapter 13

BOAL QUAY

With few exceptions, all the firm's imports of raw materials and occasional exports of products were handled through King's Lynn Docks until 1924, when a company known as Marine Traders Ltd established a wharf on the River Great Ouse at Boal Quay.

It soon became obvious to WNF directors that there were significant cost savings on transport because of the close proximity of Boal Quay to the works and the additional advantage that cargoes could be discharged directly into rail wagons and taken the short distance to the Company's own sidings by way of the harbour branch railway line. After a few years WNF obtained a controlling interest and the name of the company was changed from Marine Traders Ltd to Boal Quay Wharfingers Ltd on 5th March 1934. It was left as a separate subsidiary company. Mr A.C.K. Sheppard became secretary and director of Boal Quay Wharfingers Ltd until his death in 1949.

Main Raw Materials discharged from Boal Quay for WNF.

Phosphates: from Casablanca, Bona, Tunis, Sfax, Algiers in North Africa and Nauru Island in the Pacific.

Pyrites: from Huelva in Spain.

Potash: from Hamburg and Wismar in Germany, Antwerp in Belgium and Barcelona in Spain.

Burnt ore or ash, from the burning of pyrites to make sulphuric acid, was exported to Ghent, Antwerp and Rotterdam on the continent of Europe and Tyneside and Keadby (Scunthorpe) in this country.

Another by-product that was exported from Boal Quay was lead sulphate, known as 'sublime.' This came from the lead chambers of the sulphuric acid plants. It was shipped out in barrels, mainly to Antwerp.

In 1956/57 the first shipments of American sulphur were received. Shipments of French sulphur, from Lacq, were started in 1958/59.

Boal Quay could berth ships with a beam of 50 feet up to 350 feet in length with a draught of about 17'6" to 20' depending on tidal conditions. The largest ship ever to visit Boal Quay was the m/v Hallingdal which had a dead weight capacity of about 5,300 tons. The Hallingdal made two visits to the quay from Nauru Island in the Pacific with Nauru phosphate in bulk. On the first visit she discharged 3305 tons from 22nd to 25th February, 1937, and on the second, 3,522 tons from 1st to 4th August, 1939. On both occasions part of her cargo was discharged at another port.

In the second world war just after Dunkirk, when invasion was considered imminent, secret plans were made to remove key components from the two quayside cranes to render them immobile.

During the war, cargoes of raw materials had to be shipped in smaller coastal vessels from other ports such as Glasgow, Middlesborough, Hull, Immingham, London and Bristol.

In the 1949/50 period, the quay wall partially collapsed necessitating a lengthy period of major repairs.

The first ship to berth after the quay was rebuilt was the Foca, which discharged 1750 tons of bulk phosphate from Casablanca in June 1952.

The Sea Venture discharging phosphate, 1933.
courtesy of R Goodchild.

Chapter 14

BOSTON WORKS

The Company had considered the possibility of opening a fertiliser works at Boston in 1924, but it was not until 1930 that these plans were put into effect following the purchase of the Farina Mills in Boston, Lincs, from W. Dennis & Sons. A holding of 4.1/2% conversion stock was sold and used to purchase the property.

Cecil Sands. "I was in the gang that went to Boston Farina Mills to help modernise it into a factory. We concreted floors, knocked down walls, built new doorways, etc. We stayed in a firm's house close by. A lady came in to clean every day and the watchman did the cooking for us.

In the gang were Bob Raven, foreman bricklayer, George Bugg and myself, bricklayers, Vic Hammond, blacksmith, Bill Causton, labourer and Cecil King, watchman. We were taken to Boston by the work's van driver, Percy Tice, who was the son of Mr H. Tice, chauffeur to Dr Harry Brown."

Boston works was known by the WNF management as 'D' works. Plans were made to take bulk superphosphate by road from the works at South Lynn by a Foden steam lorry. They took delivery of this six-wheeled vehicle in 1931 (registration No. NG 361). It could carry about twelve tons of supers and operated with a trailer as well.

The first driver and fireman were Tony White and Fred Stokes respectively, and they made two deliveries a day to Boston.

The Foden steam lorry, or steamer as it became known, was involved in two accidents in 1932. In the first one it ran off the road, turned over and was "badly squashed."

In the second accident, the near side front wheel came off on the road between Hillington and Harpley and the lorry finished up in a ditch.

Boston works came into operation in 1932 and in the 1932/33 season dispatched 8,794 tons of fertilisers.

Reg Rout. "When the steamer finished, WNF bought a Foden diesel and I went to act as mate to Tony White for the two daily trips to Boston. We used to bring back bulk cement from Boston for the new housing development in Bunnett and Metcalf Avenues in South Lynn. The lorry had a rubber floor. In fact it was a wide, rubber, endless belt mounted on rollers.

This was in the days before the tipper lorries and the belt was cranked round manually by two handles to discharge the load.

We started at 7am and finished around 6pm. My wage was 16/- a week and I came in on Saturday mornings to grease up the belt rollers (there were lots of grease nipples). If this hadn't been done, the rollers would have seized up."

Boston works had a dry mixing unit and produced powdered fertiliser. In 1939, two employees were injured, one seriously, during a routine blasting operation.

The Foden steam lorry in a ditch.
courtesy of R Barham

Chapter 15

NITROGEN FERTILISERS

In 1935, WNF was making 700 tons per year of sulphate of ammonia at its plant at the old works. However, they needed considerably more than this to meet production requirements and were shipping in sulphate of ammonia mainly from Teeside and the Tyne.

At a Board meeting in 1936, a decision was taken for the Company to become self sufficient by manufacturing all the nitrogen compounds they were likely to sell. An approach was made to another fertiliser company, Messrs Fison, Packard and Prentice Ltd, and as a result a £10,000 private company was formed with the title of "Nitrogen Fertilisers."

In a press statement put out in 1937, it was mentioned that the new company would enter into a trading arrangement with the two companies concerned and that there was no question of a merger or acquisition.

George Emmerson, Mr Eric Brown's chauffeur, remembers driving the managing director to Flixborough, which was a small village north of Scunthorpe, bounded on one side by the River Trent. They got out of the car and walked into a large field and Mr Eric apparently said, "We're going to build a plant here, George."

WNF closed its sulphate of ammonia plant in 1937 and building of the new factory at Flixborough started in 1938. It eventually consisted of an ammonia plant, sulphuric acid plant and a power station, taking up 28 acres of a 56 acre site.

Lead was in short supply and WNF supplied some of the lead for the new acid plant, following the dismantling of the disused acid plant at the old works.

One of the reasons for siting the plant at Flixborough was that coke oven gas was readily available and could be supplied from a nearby steelworks by an underground pipeline. Ammonia was produced synthetically from hydrogen and nitrogen. The hydrogen was obtained by the Linde low temperature separation of coke oven gas.

As a consequence of the outbreak of the second world war, German engineers who were helping to install the plant, were forced to leave the country.

The factory was completed in 1940 and the first sulphate of ammonia was produced on 18th March 1941.

The factory was bombed on May 1941 and five men were killed. The plant was also extensively damaged and put out of action for nearly six months whilst urgent repairs were carried out.

WNF began negotiations with Fisons to sell off its shareholding interest in Nitrogen Fertilisers in February 1965.

On June 1st, 1974, the country's worst industrial explosion occurred at the Flixborough site, involving a company called Nypro Limited who were operating a chemical process on the remaining 28 acres

Chapter 16

SPRAYING ON THE FARMS

In 1934 WNF began the experimental spraying of potato crops with dilute sulphuric acid, on the theory that if the tops of the plant were killed the yield of potatoes would be increased. They also believed that the acid would kill off weeds as well as spores of fungi.

Eddy Betts. "When the season finished we went spraying; in the Spring on corn, in the Autumn on potatoes. The spraying gang included Percy Tice, Percy Ellis, Bernard Gathercole, Jack Smith and myself."

Other employees known to have undertaken spraying work included Walter Thwaite, Percy Allen and Joe Groom.

Filling the sprayer with water before adding the acid, c.1933.
courtesy of R Barham

Eddy Betts. "The spray pump worked off the wheels so the rate of spray was dependant on the speed of the horse. The sprayer held ninety gallons of water and acid from the glass carboys was added."

Eddy Betts. "On one occasion we went to Holbeach Marsh spraying potatoes. The farmer provided the horse and his horseman drove the sprayer. When we were out spraying we used to lodge with the horseman."

Offloading another type of sprayer off the Foden steam lorry. This sprayer was designed to run on a light railway track and to be pulled by a horse.

courtesy of R Barham

Chapter 17

A PASSION FOR SPORTS

It is recorded that Dr Harry Brown was a keen sportsman in his younger days and was actively associated with several local football clubs. His son Mr Eric, was an extremely enthusiastic sportsman and took an active part in the Company's sports club which was formed in 1936 and of which he was president. He was also fond of rallying and owned an Invicta sports car and prior to that an Aston Martin.

Anthony Avis. "The Invicta open tourer that he drove had an engine of tremendous capacity. In those days, petrol was delivered by hand pump and pumping even four gallons took it out of you. Well, this car held twenty gallons and the legend about it was first, it took a gallon just to warm the engine and back it out of the garage and second, he was always asked by the man at the garage, when he went to fill up, to turn off the engine as it consumed more petrol than he could pump!"

The general feeling at the time was that if you played sport you could get a job at WNF!

W.G. Gemmell. "I played hockey for the Company and also for the County A team. Before coming to work for WNF I was employed by the Railway at Magdalen and could only make the hockey team once a fortnight. When I explained this situation to Mr Eric he said there was a job for me if I applied and intimated that "something would be found."

Bill Dack. "When I came for a job interview, the second question I was asked was "Do you play football?"

The Company had become involved in providing sporting facilities for their employees in 1929, when they negotiated to obtain land for a sports field near South Lynn Railway Station. In 1936, a sports pavilion was erected by members in their own time, with WNF supplying the materials. The result was one of the finest sports grounds in West Norfolk.

Stan Hemeter. "The sporting facilities were superb and consisted of two tennis courts, a putting green, rifle range, hockey pitch, and football and cricket pitches. There were also two bowling greens which included one for the ladies. The head groundsman was Fred Brittain. His son and Stan Neale were the groundsmen. Fred always cut the bowling greens twice a day, with a hand mower."

The tennis courts, En-tout-cas, were installed in 1947.

Derek Foreman. "Mr Eric and myself were the first to play on the new tennis courts."

W.G. Gemmell. "Every section in the works played in an annual cricket and football competition. I remember 'Narny' Catton, who only played once a year, being so stiff after a game of football on the day after the match, that he had to get a sawn-down ladder in order to get into the cab of his lorry."

Eric Broad. "There were many sportsmen on the works. When the King's Lynn Angling Association team of twelve won the All-England Cup, four were employees of WNF; Ray Bocking, Len Pidgeon, Colin Stevens (Capt) and myself."

Eric Broad went on to represent England in Poland at an International Angling Event on 24.9.1961.

WNF teams, under the name of "Lynn Chemicals", played in local football leagues for many years. Several players turned out for Lynn. In 1941, their reserve football team won the Lynn Primary Cup for the second year in succession. The first eleven won the Norfolk Junior Cup in 1963 and 1966, both matches being played at Carrow Road.

For many years, up to 1960, an annual sports day was held on the sports field for employees and their families.

George Palmer. "The advent of the Lynn southern bypass spelt the end for the sports ground, however, the main bowling green, which was Cumberland turf, was lifted by machine and laid down at another sport's ground."

Top: The Domino Team, c.1950. Bottom: The Bowls Team.
courtesy of R Goodchild

104

The cricket section, c.1954.
courtesy of R Goodchild

Chapter 18

SAFETY

A visible sign of concern on safety manifested itself in 1924 when, as a result of a small fire at new works, thought to be caused by smoking, cast iron plates were made and fixed at various places bearing the notice 'Smoking strictly prohibited under penalty of instant dismissal.'

Much earlier in 1890, a more serious fire occurred at the old works, resulting in two warehouses being burnt down as well as some small sheds and a length of wooden railings beside the tow path on the River Nar. The fire was thought to be the result of a dropped lighted match. An employee spotted the fire at 9.30am on the Sunday morning and reported it to the manager. Simultaneously, a 'buzzer' was sounded at the police station. The steam and manual fire engines arrived at 10.08am and within ten minutes both engines were at work but the fire had got a strong hold and the firemen could do little other than try to prevent it spreading to other buildings. Before the arrival of the brigade, employees with buckets had attempted to get the fire under control.

At 10.25am the watching crowd were greatly excited when the shed containing nitrate of soda burst into flames with a noise like thunder. One employee rushed into the shed containing the nitrate, with the intention of carrying some of the bags to safety but was overcome by smoke and collapsed. He was rescued by a Mr W.R. Smith.

In 1923, eighteen year old Charles Knights lost part of his left forearm between the wrist and elbow when he was caught up on shafting at the dry mixing plant at the new works. The firm was prosecuted by a Factory Inspector and fined 40/- at Lynn Petty Sessions, for "failing to have a shaft on their factory properly fenced." A witness to the accident was Cyril Muncaster.

In addition to the accidents already described, (in other chapters), there were others, including one where an employee lost his right hand whilst attending a machine at the old works, in 1937.

Leonard Smith. "I had some lucky escapes. One day I was working on the floor when someone dropped a long iron bar from the floor above. It missed me by inches and stuck in the heap where I was working .

I remember once seeing a contractor working on the roof. I shouted up to him not to walk on the roof because it was made of asbestos and he would go straight through it. Half an hour later, the contractor did fall through the roof and he was very lucky. He fell on to a long timber ladder that was propped up and bounced off this straight on to a pile of sacks. He could easily have been killed.

One contractor was killed at the new works as the result of a roof fall. He was working on River Shed after there had been a frost and the roof was icy. This made him slip down the roof and fall onto the railway lines straight in front of a loco and a line of trucks."

Les Figgis. "Someone accidentally put a pick through the acid line to the den and the acid blasted up into the air only a few feet from where I was standing. I had a really lucky escape."

In 1948 Dr D.M. Dean was appointed as part time medical officer to the Company.

On 14th March 1952, Edward Baldock, a 22 year old fitter's mate was fatally injured when he was trapped in a conveyor belt at the Nar Shed.

Following this accident, George Hitch was appointed as the first full-time safety officer. George was a dedicated man and did much to lay the foundations of a safety programme. Following his retirement, through ill-health, George Howell, a prominent member of the local Red Cross as well as being one of the Company's first-aiders became acting safety officer. The author joined the safety department in April 1959 and after George Howell emigrated to Canada in November 1959, became works safety officer.

The first aid room was a little hut at the end of the work's hall, midway between the old and new works. In 1958, Sydney Goodson, who had been in charge, retired after 10 years service. He was succeeded by Phyllis Osborne who had been a Sister at the West Norfolk and King's Lynn Hospital and had considerable experience in the accident department.

P.M. Osborne. "I remember my first impression of the works and South Lynn. Everything was the same colour; the houses, the works and the mens' faces.

My first casualty was a man who had injured his foot at the top of the cranes in Nar Shed. To reach him one had to go up several vertical ladders and I can still visualise the mens' faces on the ground. "She'll never go up that ladder." But "she" did and I felt I had been accepted. I also remember my first visit to the inside of the plants. Having donned white overalls I got quite a few cat-calls of "Ices!" Again, a good friendly sign.

It was my job to visit both men and office staff who were off sick. The doctor visited the works weekly, when any problems were sorted out and anyone could be seen by him.

When I first arrived it was the beginning of the families breaking up. Grandfathers, fathers and sons, had all worked there but soon the younger ones started to break away."

Sister Osborne also trained a first aid team, holding regular weekly sessions. The work's police were a key part of this and were a great help on many occasions. Some of the members at that time were: Albert Sampson, Alf Curston, Jack Self, Bert Watson, George Brown, Fred Mason, George Dye and Jack Todd.

One such occasion occurred in an accident in March 1965, when two young steeplejacks, who had been working on crawling boards on the roof of the process building, about eighty feet above the ground, suddenly stepped onto the fragile asbestos roof sheeting and both fell through. One fell about twelve feet and hit the handrails of the granulation plant main elevator top platform and hung there on the outside of the rails, suspended only by his feet. It took all the skill of the first aid team with a Neil-Robertson stretcher to get him down to safety.

The other lad fell about sixty feet. One operator who saw him flash past thought at first it was a sack falling. He then hit a length of rubber pipe suspended by ropes. The force of the impact broke the ropes and his fall. He was then catapulted onto a concrete floor alongside one of the raw material feeders, about six feet from the ground. Both men needed hospital treatment.

P.M. Osborne. "I started in the little first aid hut which had one very small room and a 'loo.' Later it was decided to build a treatment room which was a small edition of a hospital casualty department where I could give the initial treatment before, if necessary, transferring the patient to hospital."

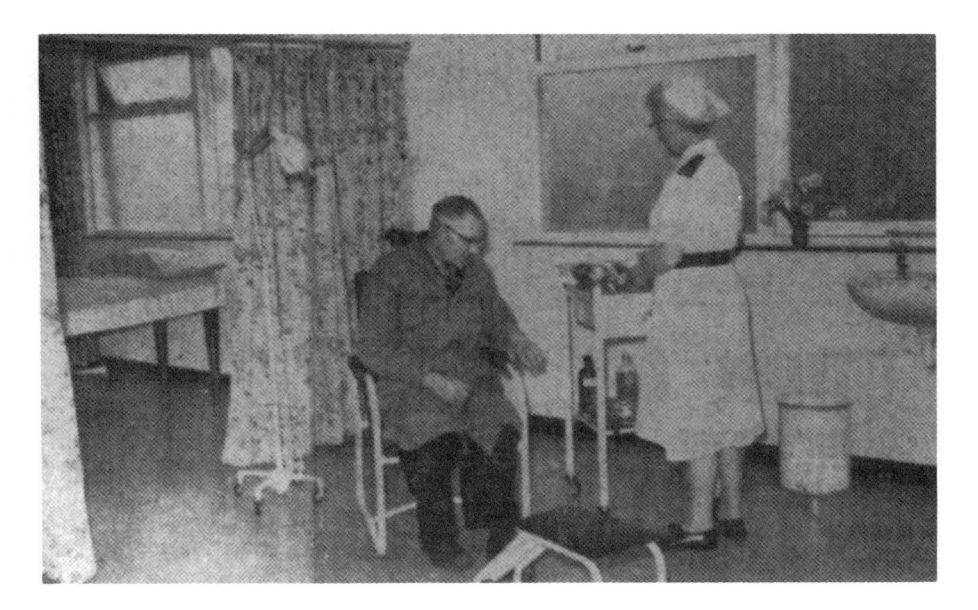

The new first aid treatment room, 1962.
Sister P.M. Osborne with Ted Oakes.

courtesy of the Lynn News

The old first aid hut became the safety equipment store, looked after by Ted Oakes. The old sack trousers and jackets had been replaced by purpose designed PVC clothing and a range of other equipment was available including gloves, goggles and safety footwear. Airline breathing apparatus was introduced for tank entry and confined space work. Ted also inspected ladders and recharged fire extinguishers.

In 1961, WNF won the Campbell Cup for the best record of industrial safety among members of Lynn and District Industrial Accident Prevention Group.

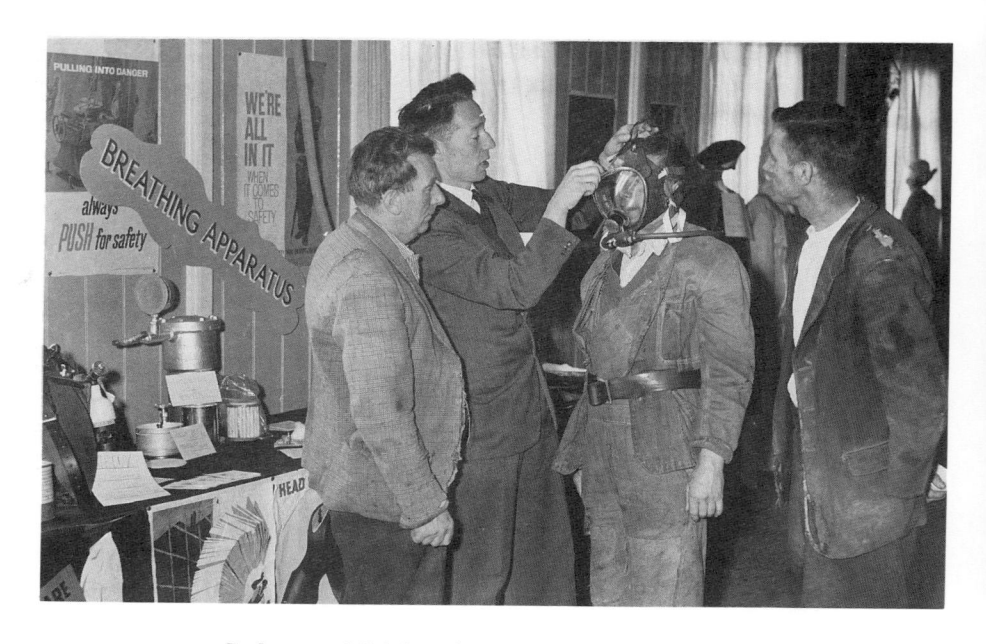

Safety exhibition in the work's hall, 1962.
L to R: 'Agga' Beales, the author, 'Nissens' Beckett, ?
courtesy of the Lynn News

On 27th March 1963 a major incident occurred, involving the release of nearly 10 tons of anhydrous ammonia. As a result, seven men were taken to hospital and eight others received treatment in the first aid centre.

It was raining in the afternoon when Alf Needham brought in a road tanker containing anhydrous ammonia from Flixborough. He positioned the tanker in the offloading bay and went to the works garage to do his paperwork. (Ammonia is a gas at normal temperature and pressure and has to be compressed for ease of transport and storage, into a liquid and held under pressure.

Harold Ward, the foreman, and Bert Yarham had inspected the flexible hoses used to offload the ammonia in the storage vessels, connected them up, opened the relevant valves and started the offloading compressor. The hoses had been designed for anhydrous ammonia duty and pressure tested but what the two men could not have seen was that one of the hoses had internal damage.

Just before 5pm this hose burst and a stream of liquid ammonia was ejected into the wet air. Almost immediately a dense, white, choking fog formed as the liquid flashed off into a gas and combined with the rain.

Stan Hemeter. "I was outside the electricians' shop talking to the lads who were getting ready to clock off, when I saw a huge bank of what looked like fog. People were walking unaware in front of it and being overtaken by it."

Derek Shears. "I had been installing floodlights with Bob Finney, on top of the ammonia tanks and had just got back to the electricians' workshop when we heard a commotion and came out to see a cloud of ammonia forming round the storage tanks and spreading out. Several of us ran to the edge of the mist and came across Joe Bennett, who was in a bad way with his face covered in blood. We ripped a door off the old pumphouse and used this as a stretcher to carry Joe to where an ambulance was waiting in Keene Road."

B(Joe)Bennett. "There were seven of us in the fitters' workshop, when suddenly there was a bang. We had the double doors at the front of the building open and suddenly a white fog of ammonia came in and you couldn't do anything. There was only one way out of the workshop and one by one everybody left except for me and Fred Massingham.

We just didn't know what to do. Suddenly the fog lifted and we could see two bodies lying on the ground in front of the acid plant. I thought, what do I do? We had a little back room with a sink and a small window. I broke the glass but it had a metal frame. I used an iron bar to try and make a space big enough but I couldn't get through, although I tried hard enough. By breaking the window I had increased the ventilation rate so even more ammonia was dragged into the workshop.

We couldn't open our mouths to talk to one another - you also couldn't open your eyes, the ammonia was so strong; you had to squint to see where you were going. Then Fred left. I took someone's mac off a peg, filled the sink in the back room with water and soaked the mac. I then put it over my head, leaving a little slit so that I could see and looked out of the door. I thought to myself, it was either stay in here and die or run out and then at least someone might see me, so that's what I did. I ran out and tripped over one of the bodies. I carried on until I reached the acid offloading tanks on the other side of the railway lines; there was a drop leading down to them and I fell into it, cutting my face. Then someone arrived in yellow protective clothing and mask and tried to revive me but I wanted to get out so I hit him. He grabbed me and dragged me through the passage way alongside the acid plant into fresh air where he laid me down on the ground. I was coughing and vomiting and then some men came running up. They pulled a door off somewhere and put me on it but I didn't remember too much after that.

I remember someone saying in the ambulance, "Poor old Joe has had it." I thought I had too. I was in hospital for two days."

Joe Bennett was rescued by Fred (Ginger) Wilson who then went back into the cloud of ammonia to lift out another man he had found on the ground in the dense white fog. After his exertions Ginger also needed treatment. He later confided, "It's alright as long as you don't breath too hard!"

Mancell Ryan. "I was in the process building, acting as a relief man on the phosphoric acid filter belt, when I saw a white cloud and saw some people waving outside. Not knowing what it was, I waved back. Then I heard somebody say it was an ammonia leak so I thought I'd better get out quick. As I started to go down the stairs I met the ammonia cloud coming up, which took my breath away. I managed to get through it, opened the door leading to the outside and collapsed into the arms of a fireman."

At the safety hut, Ted Oakes, Percy Ellis and Walter (Wacker) West, were getting ready to go home when there was a noise like escaping steam and a cloud of vapour blew out from behind the acid plant. Two men appeared out of this cloud and staggered to the river bank where one of them was violently sick. They were taken to the safety hut and a few minutes later an ambulance arrived. Both the driver and his lady attendant were wearing gas masks.

With the ambulances came the fire brigade, with Divisional Officer Norman Langley in charge. He had known what the brigade were to face when the strong smell of ammonia invaded his vehicle at the Prince of Wales roundabout.

Meanwhile, the first aid treatment room and the two adjoining offices were full of people receiving attention. Every couch was full and men were sitting on the floor propped up against the wall. The smell of ammonia hung in the air.

The Fire Brigade had brought hoses to bear on the ammonia tank which gradually became visible. Another hero emerged when Jack (Bob) Roberts, a 43 year old works maintenance foreman crawled on his stomach through the gas wearing only overalls and a gas mask for protection and closed off the main valve and stopped the leak, thus ending the incident which had lasted about thirty minutes but seemed much longer to those who have experienced it.

Jack Roberts.
courtesy of the Lynn News

In March 1964, Fred 'Ginger' Wilson was awarded the Queen's Commendation for Brave Conduct.

Chapter 19

THE 1940's-1960's EXPANSION PROGRAMME

In 1939 the directors planned to produce granulated fertiliser. Because of war shortages, steel had to be reserved, but eventually a five-tons-per-hour Sturtevant granulation plant was built at the old works in premises previously occupied by an acid plant. Mr J.C. Hovell was appointed to supervise the installation. The first trial of the plant took place in May 1945 but due to shortage of labour only one shift was possible until the end of the year.

Reg Rout. "I came back after the war and went to work as a furnaceman on the 'new' granulation plant at the old works. This was a batch plant and did about eighty-six mixings a shift. The whole production was bagged up as we made it and we finished up with about 48 tons in 1cwt paper sacks.

The plant was run from one large motor and all the driving gear, including the main shaft, was in a cage at ground floor level. Each shift had a maintenance man; on my shift it was Harry Lovick. One day he went into the cage and was caught up on the shaft; this took him round and round and he lost a leg. This would be around 1947-1948.

George Palmer. "I was transferred to the old works granulation plant. Percy Hannant was the mixer man and Reg Rout was on the furnace. The furnace was coal fired. The stoker shovelled coal into a hopper and a creeper under the hopper fed in into the furnace.

I started on the wet belt under the mixer. My duties included keeping the belt clear and making sure the material went down the chute into the revolving dryer. It frequently used to cake up. I also checked the sulphate of ammonia and muriate of potash hoppers.

Others on the same shift were Alf Canham on the tram, weighing up each batch on scales, Johnny Rose on the skip hoist which delivered the batch up to mixer floor level, Jimmy (Paddy) Boyle on the screens, Jim (Saul) Fysh on the bagging machine and Don Webber and 'Tiny' Burrows running up bags to the elevator and stacking them on an overhead gantry ready for loading.

Harry Lovick was the maintenance man and one day I saw him get caught up by the main driving shaft in the motor cage. He had apparently leaned over the rotating driving shaft and he got caught up and was taken round and round by the shaft. His left leg was continually hitting the concrete pedestal on which the equipment was mounted.

You got a certain bonus if you did eighty six mixings. You then cleaned out and got ready for the next shift. The mixer or granulator was a rotating pan and did one batch at a time. (This was an "Eirich" mixer). You timed in so much water and you had to get it right. It would come out of the dryer like dust if you didn't put enough water on or like sludge if you put on too much. I kept a record for the different types of mixings."

The old works granulation plant, c. 1950. George Hitch, the foreman, is on the right.

courtesy of Mr R Goodchild

Earlier, the managing director had examined the possibility of manufacturing concentrated fertiliser, using triple superphosphate by reacting phosphate rock with phosphoric acid instead of sulphuric acid.

The expansion programme began to gather momentum. Increased demand for granular fertiliser required more production capacity. Mr Eric Brown went to Sweden to visit Sven Nordengrin and look at plans for producing phosphoric acid and for making granular fertiliser by a continuous process. The outcome was the planned installation of a thirty-five-tons-per-hour granulation plant and a phosphoric acid plant, both designed by Sven Nordengrin.

A process building, 90 feet high and with an unsupported width of 200 feet, was designed to hold these plants, plus an additional plant to produce concentrated granular fertiliser.

Also placed on order, was a sulphuric acid plant, increased raw material storage and a new product storage warehouse. Called 'Nar Shed' it was designed to store 35,000 tons of bulk granular product in bays, complete with two overhead electric travelling cranes, two, forty ton per hour bagging machines and both road and rail loading facilities.

Process foremen had already begun a shift working routine .

Eric Broad. "After demob from the RAF I joined WNF in 1946 and started as a foreman learning the job with Billy Clitheroe, who was the senior shed foreman on the old works. The other two foremen were George Hitch and Frank King. I followed Billy around for a week and this was considered the training for the job. When I knew the operation, I was moved to the new works with Bill Vaughan, on days, and they seemed very long days.

I then went on shift to look after both old and new works. The shifts were 6-2, 2-10 and 10-6 and there were three of us, Fred Dunbabin, George Howell and myself. We worked seven days a week with no days off. For some reason, the only shift we didn't work was the 2-10 on the Sunday, when the Moritz den crew used to come in and wash out the scrubbers.

In the early 1950's there were four shift foremen; myself, Fred Dunbabin, Peter Morley and Bill Sampson. (George Howell came off shiftwork to become the foreman on River Shed). Hours were reduced from 48 to 42.

I married in 1950 and moved to a firm's house at 163, Saddlebow Road, which was next to the new works office, a Nissen hut.

When the new office block was built, my house and the adjoining property, also owned by WNF, were demolished. I shared an office with Bill Vaughan and realised when I looked out of the window that my new office was in exactly the same position as the front room in my old house had been!"

In 1949, work began on preparing the ground for the new buildings.

Alf Needham. "Hogging was brought from Wendling for the Nar Shed foundations, with three Canadian Ford V.8 tippers. The drivers were George Moyse, Narny Catton and Ivan Fincham."

Bert Dye. "I went into the 'heavy gang' and helped prepare the site for the new process building. Before we started levelling, the site was mainly allotments with a pit in the middle. We also put drains in. I remember working in a trench one day when somebody dropped a brick on my head!

George Fisher was in charge of the gang. It was also known as 'Fisher's gang. Others were: Horry Marsters, Ted Neale, Bill Bannister, Sid Pooley, Taffy Dowell, Percy Grimes, (who drove a tractor, then a small calf dozer) and Bert Wain, who drove a tractor and trailer.

I also helped to cart brick rubble from a camp at Mundford. We used to knock down disused hut walls and load the rubble, bringing it back for the Nar Shed site."

Pile driving started in September 1949. A total of 395 piles were used in the foundations of the process building; the majority of these were 55 feet in length and weighed over five tons each.

A tidal flood in 1949 caused flooding of the Nar Shed site.

The process building foundations taking shape.

courtesy of R Goodchild

The steelwork for the new process building was brought down from Sheffield where it had been used as a wartime blackout over a blast furnace.

Tom Snape. "When the big process building was being built, I had to sit on a steel stanchion at the top of the building, to direct the crane. I just climbed up there and sat on the top. The people who put up the steelwork could walk across a 2" girder without turning a hair. They told me the signals to give to the crane driver."

As the process building was taking shape, raw material stores of a parabolic design were being constructed for pyrites and sulphate of ammonia. Also being installed was a system of belt conveyors so that raw materials could be fed into hoppers, inside the process building using tractor shovels.

The large new storage warehouse, called Nar Shed, was built on the east side of the River Nar and a concrete bridge was constructed to give both road and rail access.

Nar shed.
courtesy of R Goodchild

The first plant to be completed in the new process building was the thirty -tons- per-hour granulation plant.

Reg Rout. "I was transferred to the new granulation plant as a furnaceman and was the first to light up the oil-fired furnace and start up the plant, which was a continuous operating plant rather than a batch operation."

George Palmer. "When the new granulation plant was ready I went over as a granulator man. Compound, pre-mixed in a rotating drum, was fed into a large horizontal, slightly inclined revolving granulator and sprayed with water. I had a water meter to help judge how much was needed. Scrapers had to be put on regularly to remove build-up from the sides of the granulator.

The plant could produce approximately 900 tons in a twenty four hour operation, the production going from the process building to the Nar Shed via one of two rubber conveyor belts that went high over the River Nar. Maintenance was on a Monday morning ready for the afternoon shift to start up. The screens were designed to be periodically shut-down and cleaned while the operation was going on. The throughput was high, in order to achieve 35-40 tons per hour of product. Occasionally, the main elevator, taking all the material from the dryer and up onto the high level screens, would be blocked due usually to a piece of scale lodged in the down chute and a cascade of material would rapidly form a huge heap of spillage on the floor. Feeding in spillage was a full-time job."

The granulation plant in operation.
courtesy of R Goodchild

George Palmer. "The granulator operator started up the plant which had all its equipment driven by individual motors, a change from the past. Blasts were given on a klaxon to warn people to stand clear of the belts and other moving equipment."

New Shed showing heaps of superphosphate.
courtesy of R Goodchild

The phosphoric acid plant was also installed in the process building, much of it being fabricated in the workshop.

George Palmer. "Phosphate rock and sulphuric acid were to be reacted together in a mixer, then fed into the first of four lead-lined timber reaction vessels. The vessels were made on the barrel principle with pitch pine staves being shaped with an adze. The whole construction was held together with steel bands bolted together on the outside."

Jack Adcock. "Tom Snape and myself helped to fit the supporting steelwork for the reaction vessel stirrers. The vessels were over 17 feet across and had lead-lined pitch pine stirrers inside. The drive for this consisted of a motor and a bevel pinion gear wheel driving a large crown wheel."

On the 31st January, 1953, while the phosphoric acid plant was still under construction, the great flood occurred.

The Author. "I was the foreman on the 3-11 shift. The first indication that there might be trouble was when Eric Broad, who was off duty, came and told me that there was a high tide and to make sure the Nar sluice valve was shut, otherwise the new works den would be flooded. I went over to the den and found that the miller had already done this. While I was there I went to look at the Nar and found that the river was almost level with the top of the banks. Inside River Shed, water was starting to pour through the wall like so many taps. The granulation plant was shut down so I brought all the men over to River Shed where we tried, in vain, to stem the various streams of water. We stacked bags full of fertiliser against the wall but it made little difference. Word came to us that the Great Ouse had flooded. We got back into the process building and had just made the safety of the first floor of the granulation plant when the main floodwater arrived in the process building and all the lights went out leaving us in total darkness. A gang of contract lead burners had been working on the phosphoric acid plant lining the vessels. They made their welding torches into improvised flares. By the flickering light of these, I suddenly became aware that there was a group of people with them. I later learnt that they had left their homes in Saddlebow road to take refuge in the process building.

I left the process building by way of the twin belts to see what was happening on the rest of the works. There was a junction along the twin belt conveyor walkway that was called 'Charing Cross', that led to the new works den. I took this route and made my way to the works hall which had escaped the flood. Here, a group of employees had been enjoying their regular Saturday night whist game. They included Edgar Broad, the works manager, who had left his car at Black Shed at the old works, which was at a much lower level. When we got there the car roof was just visible above the murky water. At that moment I remembered that I had left my shoes in the office alongside Saddlebow road! I found them the next morning. John Williamson had thoughtfully put all the shoes on top of a high cupboard, before evacuating the building."

Early next morning the big clean-up started and a race to get electric motors serviced, pits pumped out and tons of flood-contaminated fertiliser removed. One of the worst jobs was in the sulphate of ammonia store. There was a conveyor in an underground tunnel that went the length of the store. This had to be cleaned out and men toiled down there by the light of hurricane lamps in intense cold in an atmosphere reeking with ammonia.

The aftermath of the flood at the old works granulation plant.
courtesy of R Goodchild

The new works granulation plant restarted production on the 12th February with the rest of the plants starting at intervals until early March. The lead chamber plant, as mentioned in chapter 8, did not restart. Problems caused by the flooding continued to plague the granulation plant for several months.

Meanwhile the phosphoric acid and new sulphuric acid plants were up and running. Both were continuous processes. On the phosphoric acid plant, ground phosphate rock was treated with sulphuric acid to produce a slurry.

George Palmer. "The hot acidic slurry made in the reaction vessels was pumped back to a vacuum cooler and then recycled through the reaction vessels until finally being pumped up onto the filter belt. This was a Lanskrona continuous belt filter under vacuum and the acid was sucked out of the slurry through a filter cloth leaving a cake consisting of gypsum. This was taken and tipped into a disused sandpit at Leziate; prior to this the gypsum had been dumped on the Nar field. As refinements were added, the belt filter was changed to a rotating" Prayon" tray filter. Acid was collected in open-topped lead lined vessels below.

One day, the top of one of the reaction vessels fell in. I had been on top of this vessel five minutes previous to it falling in. On another occasion, one of the reaction vessels burst. The steel bands broke and when this happened the vessel could no longer support the weight of the slurry, (it contained around 66 tons) so it burst open and a large quantity of hot slurry came out and caused flooding right across the floor. All the drains and the sump pit on the ground floor were covered with wooden slats (steel would have rapidly corroded) and these all lifted up and floated away. One of the fitters entered the plant by a side door and unaware of the catastrophe, stepped inside and right into a deep drain full of slurry. Fortunately he escaped without injury.

I remember one Sunday morning when everything was going well. Someone had gone out to get the papers and the filter belt and mixer operators were both reading these when the general manager, A.I. Coleman, walked in. He said to me, "If a workman is reading a newspaper and the foreman is smoking a pipe (which I was at the time) then I know everything is alright, but God help you if it isn't!"

A "Lopulco" mill, (quickly named the 'lollipop' mill) was installed close to the phosphate store and the ground phosphate was conveyed to the phosphoric acid plant by a "Fuller-Kinyon" conveyor system that discharged the material into a silo, adjacent to the mixing section.

Ken Nurse. "One day the silo blocked up so the slide at the bottom of the discharge chute was fully opened. Suddenly the blockage cleared itself and a large quantity of phosphate poured out like water. It couldn't be stopped and soon covered the conveyor and feeder underneath. It took two days to clear it all up.

One of my worst moments was when the pipeline from the phosphoric acid plant sump pit burst and I got acid in my eyes. After washing my eyes with water, I insisted on going home to change into clean underwear before going to hospital. I couldn't see. I woke up in hospital and still couldn't see. I thought I was blind. My eyelids were stuck to my eyeballs. The sister managed to free them and suddenly I could see daylight but everything was blurred."

While the new contact sulphuric acid plant was being constructed a worldwide shortage of sulphur existed, hence the decision to continue to use Spanish iron pyrites. The new plant was unique in that it used Freeman Nichols flash roasters to burn the ore. These where the first of their kind to be installed in this country. The pyrites ore first had to be dried and ground in a ball mill. This finely pulverised material was then blown into hot combustion chambers and burned to produce sulphur dioxide. The process gave off surplus heat which was utilised to produce steam in boilers.

The Ball Mill.
courtesy of R Goodchild

Up until 1956, the plant had been using mainly iron pyrites known as Rio Tinto confines. In 1956 the first shipment of American sulphur was received. This was very pure and required no treatment to remove dust and impurities. It was melted with steam coils and the resultant molten sulphur was injected into the roasters in atomised form. Shipments of French sulphur from Lacq started in 1958.

Fires with sulphur were very common but were usually easily dealt with.

Bill Dack. "When we were working in the sulphur pits Cyril Sedgewick used to stand by with a bucket of water . This was because the sulphur caught fire very easily. You would hardly be aware it was on fire until you saw the blue flame and the sulphur turning black."

There were occasional problems when the plant had to start up following a shut down, particularly when it was raining. This led to complaints from householders and gardeners of damage to curtains and crops. To lessen the impact of any further problems a new chimney was installed; at 170 feet high it was twice as tall as the previous chimney.

While the acid plant was operating with finely ground pyrites, the resultant ash was sprayed with water in equipment called the pug mill and shipped out in rail wagons.

After the end of the second world war, a pilot plant was installed in the old works boiler house for experiments in connection with the manufacture of concentrated fertiliser, using triple superphosphate.

The Author. "I started in the laboratory in April 1950. My first morning was spent in the pilot plant which was operating at the time with Joe Sizeland, Jimmy Boyle and Stan Bussey. Charley Edwards was the fitter. (He was also the secretary of the cricket section). Taking samples were Graham English and Lionel Francis. The former, wearing an old white mac tied up with a piece of string, was in charge of the small research laboratory which was attached to the main laboratory.

I was in the pilot plant one day when the managing director, Mr Eric Brown came in. He was wearing a very smart suit. To my astonishment he took off his jacket, picked up a shovel and went to work. A week later I received a second surprise. I opened a letter. 'Dear Bill, Would you like to play cricket for my eleven on Sunday? Eric.' No one in authority had ever called me 'Bill' before."

The pilot plant, c. 1950.
courtesy of R Goodchild

Mr Eric had been personally involved in the new process which was known as the Brown/Standaert process.

From the work done in the small-scale pilot plant, the twelve-tons-per-hour CM (Concentrated Manure) plant was designed and built in the process building. The installation was carried out by Barry, Henry and Cook of Aberdeen. Several employees were involved in the actual construction.

George Palmer. "I helped to build the CM plant. A big Scotsman called Jock Walker was the contract foreman in charge of the building programme. When he said, "Bring a wee sticky up here," he was talking about a scaffold board!

The Author. "Three shifts were formed to run the new plant and three of the shift process foremen, Eric Broad, Peter Morley and myself, took one shift each for a seven day a week commissioning period that lasted for nine months. On my shift were S('Nod')Nicholls, Harry Simpson, Nevil Senter, Bill Loasby and Herbert Neve.

The usual teething problems were encountered which included mechanical breakdowns, blockages and continuous spillage of material."

The CM plant was a successful venture. At the Annual General Meeting for 1954, it was mentioned that concentrated fertiliser of high quality had been introduced.

In 1955 a development department was established to plan and co-ordinate future projects. Henry Kidd was put in charge of a small team of engineers who were located at Number 9, Nelson Street (see chapter 11). The two houses owned by the Company opposite the main office on Wisbech Road, 'Narside' and 'White Gables', were also used by the development department.

One of the projects was the manufacture of ammonium phosphate, using anhydrous ammonia and phosphoric acid.

The anhydrous ammonia was brought in by road tanker and offloaded into pressure storage vessels.

George Palmer. "Between the granulation and phosphoric acid plants was the slurry tank where ammonium phosphate was made. The slurry was then sprayed onto the compound in the granulator. By this time the granulation plant at the old works had been shut down."

A new project, veiled in secrecy, had been started, to produce granular concentrated fertiliser by a fluidised bed technique, where air is blown through holes in a plate floor at sufficient velocity to lift all the particles of solid matter and result in the whole bed of material being fluidised, ie, to resemble water when it is boiling. The theory was that the mixing, coating, drying and size separation could all be done whilst the material was in this fluidised state.

The Author. "In 1956 I joined the development department to work with David Little, a chemical engineer, on project 5008, which was the code name for the fluidised bed process. A building next to the old works mill had been put aside for a pilot plant and I spent several weeks experimenting with a 4" glass reactor trying to fluidise fertiliser granules and obtain the optimum air velocity rates and pressure drops.

The pilot plant crew consisted of Harry Hooks, who looked after the outside boiler, Paul Ryan, Charley Rodwell, Tom Taylor and Alfie Panton, the last two doing the plumbing and fitting respectively.

This operation lasted for over two years until eventually we were able to run the pilot plant on twelve hour shifts."

Meanwhile, back in the production department, changes were taking place in the granulation plant operation.

John Williamson. "I had become an assistant plant manager with Eric Broad, Peter Morley and Bill Vaughan. We went on shift to try and boost production. The highest rate achieved was 960 tons in twenty four hours on No. 17 special compound.

The old premixer on the granulation plant was eventually dispensed with and was used to mix the granules with china clay to stop them sticking together. Oil was heated up and sprayed into the mixer under pressure through a nozzle. The china clay would then stick to the granules. One day we had a problem and I went into the mixer to investigate. Suddenly the nozzle that had been blocked became unblocked and I was literally coated with a spray of hot oil."

The new fluidised bed plant was built in place of the CM plant, which was now redundant, and produced concentrated fertilisers known as MAP5 and MAP6. Its operation, however, was beset with difficulties and was never really successful. It also had a high power consumption.

A welcome change to the bucket of water and sack towel washing facilities and equally primitive changing facilities came in 1962, when the new office and welfare block was opened at the new works. To accommodate the new building, the old Nissen hut offices alongside the Saddlebow road were demolished as were two adjoining company houses.

The new premises housed offices, a quality control laboratory, canteen, locker rooms, washing and shower facilities and a comprehensive first aid section.

New offices were also built at the old works in the courtyard between the offices fronting Wisbech road and the Nissen huts.

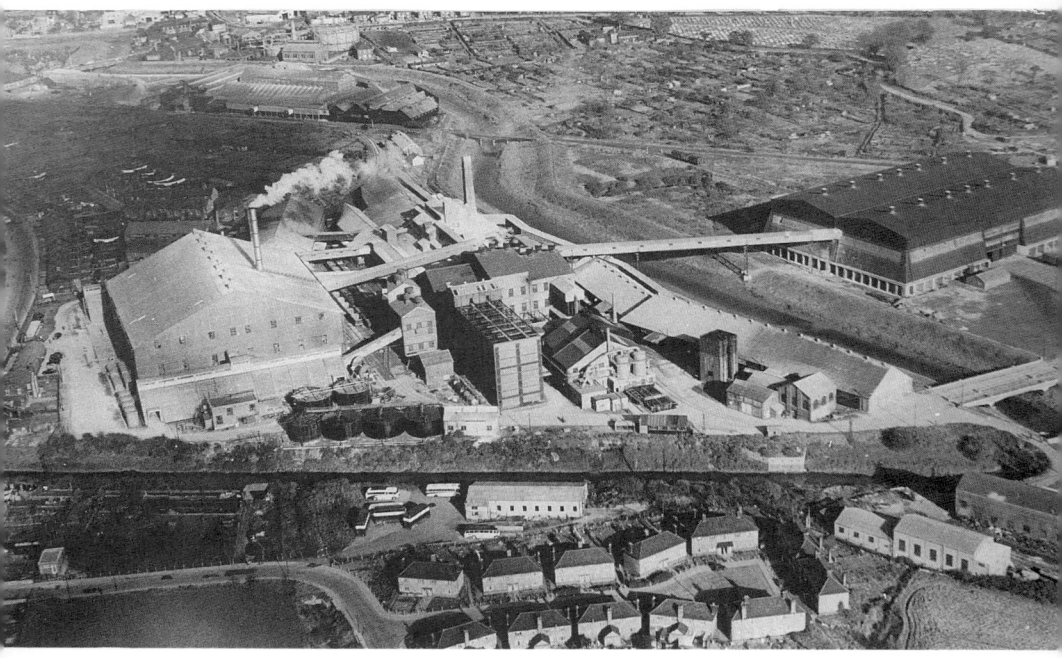

Aerial view of the site, c.1953.
courtesy of Hydro Agri (UK) Limited

Chapter 20

FINALE

The year ending 30th June 1963 resulted in a trading loss of around £90,000 for the Company and is believed to be their first ever loss.

A further loss was sustained in the following year.

One of the reasons given for the 1963 loss, was the long commissioning period of the new granulation plant, which was beset with teething problems.

In January 1963, an initiative was launched to increase sales in various parts of the country by trying to sell direct to farmers at a reduced price and to guarantee delivery on set dates. A number of staff, including the author, were seconded to this venture.

During 1964 the directors made a decision to seek help in running the Company because of increased sales competition and increasing technical advances in fertiliser manufacture.

Prior to this, they had looked into the possibility of buying ammonium nitrate, but the cost of converting the granulation plant to handle this product was considered to be prohibitive.

Their next step was to negotiate with "Leathers Chemicals" of Bradford, who had the technical expertise, the deal being that WNF would purchase "Leathers Chemicals" issued shares, in return for WNF shares. By this merger, the chairman of "Leathers" would become the managing director. This was agreed between the two parties involved and the Co-operative Wholesale Society, who owned half the shares in WNF.

To obtain approval for the transaction it was necessary to hold an extraordinary meeting of shareholders, giving them the mandatory twenty one days notice. During this period Fisons bid for the shares in the Company, making an offer to purchase all the ordinary WNF £1 shares at 30/- each.

On the 5th April, 1965, the shareholders, led by the Co-operative Wholesale Society, voted against the proposed merger thereby extinguishing the "WNF/Leathers" agreement.

Subsequently, the directors of "Leathers" sued the Co-operative Wholesale Society for breach of agreement and the judge found in their favour, awarding damages and costs. In the course of the hearing, both parties acknowledged that Fisons had not at any time acted improperly in the takeover of WNF.

Prior to the attempted merger with "Leathers", 26 staff and 45 works employees were made redundant as part of a cost-saving exercise.

D.G. Jary and W.N. Ashby retired on 15.1.1965, after which four employees were given early retirement; these were H.M. Carnall, A.E. Coupland, B.J. Riches and R.H. Brown, who was only six months short of 50 years service.

John Batch. "Reg Brown was one of the most loyal servants WNF ever had and put in many hours of his own time without thought of payment. He told me, "I would have worked for nothing to get the 50 years in."

West Norfolk Fertilisers continued as a subsidiary of Fisons. In 1967, production of chemical fertilisers ceased and an announcement was made that 240 people were to become redundant. In addition, Boal Quay was closed down and arrangements made to dispose of a major part of the 50 acre WNF site.

What was left of the site continued for a time, mainly as a store and the name was changed to Fisons.

West Norfolk Fertilisers was finally wound up as a Company on 30th April, 1982.

INDEX

Abel A.W. 15, 31.
Adcock J. 24.
Adcock Jack. 84, 85, 89, 121.
Adcock Eddy. 90, 91,92.
Ainger. 21.
Allen Derek. 87.
Allen Percy. 47, 100.
Allflatt John. 92.
Anger. 10.
Anger J. 11.
Anger R. 12.
Appleton J. 12, 37.
Arnold C. 11.
Arrowsmith Matt. 66.
Arrowsmith T.W. 28, 66.
Ashby A. 11.
Ashby Charley. 49.
Ashby J.W. 28.
Ashby W.N. 132.
Athey J. 14.
Avis. 10.
Avis Anthony. 30, 102.
Avis H. 13.
Avis W. 12.
Baldock Edward. 107.
Bannister Bill. 117.
Barber Peter. 48.
Barker Cecil. 64.
Barker Harry. 44.
Barnaby W. 27, 85.
Barnard A. 13.
Barnes F.W. 11.
Barrett Bill. 64.
Barrett T. 27, 75.
Barron A.E. 14, 29, 77.
Barron Les. 87.
Bass. 21.
Bass H. 24, 54.
Batch John. 88, 132.
Baugh Dave. 84.
Baxter Bill. 77, 78.
Beales 'Agga.' 74, 75, 110.
Beck Horace. 6.
Beckett 'Nissens'. 87, 110.
Bedwell Gordon. 83.
Bedwell W. 27, 83, 84.
Beevus Charley. 42.
Benefer 'Biddy.' 64.
Bennett B (Joe) 68, 111, 112.
Bennington T. 31.

Berry Lew. 44.
Betts Charles. 6.
Betts Eddy. 44, 47, 49, 86, 100, 101.
Betts William. 6.
Bird J.M. 6,
Blomfield William. 6.
Bloom. 21.
Bocking H. 31.
Bocking Ray. 103.
Bone Mrs. 879.
Booer Siddy. 57.
Bowman S. 27.
Boxall Chris. 80,81.
Boyle Jimmy (Paddy) 114, 126.
Bramham Frank. 49.
Bramham Pat. 41, 44.
Brereton George. 6.
Brittain Ernest. 61, 62.
Brittain Fred. 103.
Broad Edgar. 14, 31, 32, 80, 82, 122.
Broad Eric. 57, 67, 103, 168, 124, 127, 129.
Brooks Les. 15, 90, 91, 92.
Brown A.E. 27.
Brown E. 15.
Brown Edith. 23, 77, 78.
Brown Enid. 23.
Brown E.H.I.(Mr Eric). 25, 27, 30, 31, 63, 72, 88, 98, 102, 103, 116, 126, 127.
Brown George. 108.
Brown G.R. (George). 15, 21, 27, 61.
Brown H.C. (Dr Harry). 18, 19, 23, 25, 31, 38, 63, 72, 78, 79,90, 96, 102.
Brown H.H. 14, 23, 28, 45.
Brown James. 6, 18, 23, 28, 77.
Brown J.S. (Joe). 14, 23, 28, 29, 77, 78, 79.
Brown John. 5.
Brown R.H. (Reg). 25, 27, 88, 89, 91, 132.
Brown Thomas. 5, 6, 17, 19, 22.
Bugg George. 96.
Bunn Jim. 71.
Bunting Henry. 84.
Burden Ernie. 64.
Burling H. 13.
Burling W. 12.
Burrows A. 27.
Burrows T. 27.
Burrows 'Tiny.' 114.
Burton Mrs. 31.
Bush Elwyn. 81.
Bussens Cliff. 88.

Bussey Stan. 126.
Calton Elizah. 23.
Canham Alf. 114.
Calton J. 11.
Carnall H.M. 132.
Cassell. 10.
Castle R. 12.
Castle R. (Dick). 27, 84, 85.
Caston. 9.
Catton Mrs A.L. 26.
Catton E. 13.
Catton 'Horry.' 75.
Catton Lenny. 75.
Catton 'Narny.' 75, 103, 117.
Catton W.J. 31.
Causton Bill. 96.
Chapman F. 12.
Chase M. 31.
Chatten F. 27.
Childs David. 87..
Chilvers Fred. 87..
Clark. 21.
Clark 'China.' 48, 74, 75.
Clark Doris. 52.
Clark Peter. 75.
Clarke A.H. 25.
Claydon W.G. 31.
Clitheroe. 21.
Clitheroe Bill. 43, 116.
Clitheroe G. 27.
Clitheroe George. 85.
Clitheroe G.W. 28.
Coleman A.I. 31, 32, 124.
Collison Maisie. 52.
Collison Millie. 52.
Colquhoun Duncan. 84, 85.
Colquhoun Joyce. 92.
Cook Lenny. 87.
Cooke L. 27.
Cooper. 21.
Coston Doug. 85.
Coupland A.E. 132.
Cox W. 31, 32, 90, 91, 92.
Craven P. 32.
Crowther 'Bubbles.' 85.
Curry P. 89.
Curson. 9.
Curson J. 11.
Curston Alf. 88, 108.
Curtis Alf. 86.
Cutting Percival. 14.
Dack Bill. 84, 102, 126.

Daisley E. 28.
Daisley F. 12.
Dans. 10.
Davis. 9, 10.
Dawson H. 27.
Day Bill. 85.
Day T. 11.
Dean. 10.
Dean Dr D.M. 68, 107.
Denny Tom. 84.
Dent Vera. 52.
Dewart Graham. 87.
Dickerson Alfred. 21.
Dinnage Reg. 87.
Dixon. 12.
Dowell 'Taffy.' 117.
Dunbabin Fred. 27, 116.
Durrant A. 19.
Dyble S. 24.
Dye. 9.
Dye Bert. 75, 85, 117.
Dye George. 108.
Easton A.E. 31.
Edge. 21.
Edgeley George. 85.
Edgeley Ron. 85.
Edwards A. 31.
Edwards Charley. 126.
Eggett E. 13.
Eglen Dick. 49, 83.
Ellis Albert. 75.
Ellis B. 19.
Ellis Derek. 85.
Ellis. Gordon. 87.
Ellis John B. 6.
Ellis Percy. 75, 100, 112.
Elms L. 30, 79.
Elms Stanley. 78, 79, 80.
Elms W. 27.
Emmerson George, 98.
English G. 24.
English Graham. 90, 126.
Evans G. 11.
Farr J. 11.
Farrow. 9.
Fawkes Bill. 38, 40, 41, 42, 43, 44, 47, 54, 75.
Fayers. 21.
Fayers R. 28.
Fenn H.J. (Bertie) 14, 26, 27, 41.
Figgis Les. 34, 35, 38, 43, 44, 45, 46, 49, 55, 56, 57, 58, 70, 71, 73, 107.

Fincham Ivan. 75, 117.
Finney Bob. 87, 111.
Fish. 10.
Fish Albert. 75.
Fisher A.G. 31.
Fisher George. 87, 117.
Fitzgerald J. 15.
Flintham Bill. 80.
Foreman. 10.
Foreman Derek. 37, 77, 79, 103.
Foreman F. 14.
Francis Lionel. 90, 126.
Fretwell B. 24.
Frost Harry. 42.
Frost Jack. 61, 63.
Fryer A.J. 14.
Fuller R. 12.
Funnell Fred. 75.
Fysh. 10.
Fysh H .(Harry). 27, 54, 57.
Fysh J.W. (Jim) 31, 32, 54, 114.
Fysh T. 11.
Gamble Doug. 64.
Gamble F. 14.
Gamble John. 75.
Gamble 'Yoggy.' 75.
Gant Fred. 85.
Garne. 10.
Garrod Hector. 64, 87.
Gathercole Bernard. 40, 44, 49, 62, 100.
Gayton W. 13.
Gemmell W.G. 73, 74, 79, 102, 103.
Ghem H. 13.
Ghem P. 11.
Golden W. 14.
Golden W.F. 29.
Goldsmith. 9, 13.
Goodson S.J. (Sidney). 31, 107.
Gore J. 27.
Grainger A. 11
Graver Peter. 87.
Green Wally. 44.
Greenacre Jack. 49.
Griffiths Peter. 87.
Griggs George. 71.
Grimes Percy. 117.
Groom. 10.
Groom J. (Joe). 27, 87, 100.
Guymer W. 11.
Hall Pat. 87.
Hall Edgar. 6.
Hammond. 22.

Hammond George. 44.
Hammond Vic. 96.
Hammond Wm. 14, 29, 79.
Hampson Mary. 78.
Hancock W. 11.
Hannant Percy. 114.
Hanwell H. 11.
Hardy. 21.
Hardy G. 24.
Hardy Jack. 49.
Hardy John. 15.
Harris Bill. 77.
Harris Bob. 85.
Harrod F.W. 12.
Hart. 21.
Harvey. 21.
Harvey R. 11.
Haverson J. 12.
Hawkshaw J.M. 61, 65.
Hemeter Stan. 87, 88,102, 111.
Hendry. 21.
Hewitt Chas. 13.
Hewitt H. 13.
Hickman Arthur. 86.
Hickman A.E. 31.
Hides. 9.
Hiel. 9.
Hiel T. 12.
Hildon J. 26.
Hill. 9, 10.
Hill H. 27.
Hill John. 89.
Hill R.R. 13, 14, 24, 26.
Hitch George. 107, 115, 116.
Hodd Billy. 79..
Holdgate. 9.
Holmes George. 86.
Hooks H. (Harry). 31, 129.
Hornigold Les. 49.
Horseley 'Ossie.' 87.
Hovell J.C. 31, 114.
Howard Sid. 84.
Howell George. 107, 116.
Howlett Dora. 52.
Howlett Fred. 75.
Howlett Lily. 52.
Howlett Violet. 52.
Howlett W.J. 41, 44, 45.
Howling Maude. 51, 52.
Hudson A.E. 31.
Human Cliff. 79.
Hurn. 21.

Ives Albert Charles. 42.
Jackson B. 12.
Jarvis. 21.
Jarvis W. 27.
Jary. D.G. (Dave). 43, 84, 88, 132.
Jary Mary. 51, 52.
Johnson. 10.
Johnson George, 87.
Johnson James B. 14.
Jones Clifford. 87.
Jopling Len. 85.
Jordan 'Dubby.' 75.
Jubey G.W. (George). 27, 60, 61, 64.
Kay J. 14.
Ketteringham W. (Billy). 27, 85.
Kidd H.C. (Henry). 32, 89, 128.
King C. 27.
King Cecil. 96.
King Frank. 116.
Kirk Wilf. 85.
Knights Charles. 106.
Knowles Peter, 87.
Knowles Herbie. 57.
Lake F. 27.
Lake George. 45.
Lake Nellie. 52.
Lake T. 24.
Lake W. 28.
Lammiman Alf. 74.
Lane Alfie. 83.
Langley Norman. 112.
Latus Alf. 85.
Laws George. 27.
Lawson Jack. 63.
Lee B. 12, 13.
Lee Captain Jack. 38.
Leech Lance. 90, 92.
Leverington C. 14.
Libbey R.P. 32, 80, 90.
Linford L. 27.
Little David. 89, 128.
Loasby Bill. 128.
Lovick Harry. 114, 115.
Luckly J. 11.
Ludkin Molly. 52.
Luther Martin. 78.
Lynn. 21.
Lyon Maisie. 52.
Mace Herbert. 75.
Main Albert. 64.
Manning. 21.
Manning C. 27.

Manning Jack. 49.
Marchant Fred. 87.
Marriott Stan. 87.
Marsters 'Horry.' 73, 117.
Marsters P. (Percy). 27, 44.
Mason Fred. 108.
Massen Edie. 52.
Massen Harry. 44.
Massingham Fred. 111.
Massingham Matt. 64.
Mawby A.J. 31.
Mawby Jack. 83.
Mawby Joe. 57.
Mawby T. 13.
Mayer Andy. 85.
Mayes George. 87.
McHale P.J. 32.
McKenna Jim. 84.
McKenna Mick. 84.
Medlock. 9, 10, 13.
Medlock W. 11.
Mennell. 21.
Mitchell. 12.
Mitchell A. 24, 31.
Mitchell Arthur. 84.
Mitchell Joe. 45, 49, 75.
Moore. 10.
Morgan F.W. 14, 19.
Moritz Rene. 63.
Morley Peter. 92, 116, 127, 129.
Morrison. 13.
Moyse George. 75, 117.
Muncaster Cyril. 106.
Mussett Madge. 78.
Neal Geo. 13.
Neale. 21.
Neale Stan. 103.
Neale Ted. 117.
Needham Alf. 50, 75, 110, 117.
Needham Mrs E. 52.
Nelson Gordon. 92.
Neve Herbert. 128.
Newby J.G. 29, 32, 79.
Nicholls 'Nod.' 75.
Nicholls S. 128.
Nicholls Walter. 75.
Nicholls W.W. 31.
Nordengrin Sven. 116.
Nunn J. 13.
Nurse Ken. 64, 68, 125.
Nurse Mrs W.N. 77.
Oakes. 21.

Oakes E. 11
Oakes Florrie. 52.
Oakes H. 13.
Oakes J. 12.
Oakes R. 12.
Oakes Sidney. 69, 74, 75.
Oakes Ted. 109, 112.
Oldfield Alfred. 6, 18.
Osborne Sister P.M. 107, 108, 109.
Otterspoor Madge. 78.
Overson J. 12.
Padget G. 11.
Palmer Dorothy. 34.
Palmer F. 24.
Palmer George. 46, 103, 146, 119, 120, 121, 124, 127, 128.
Palmer 'Snowy.' 54.
Palmer Walter. 34.
Panton Alf. 64, 68, 129.
Parnell C. 21.
Parnell G. 21.
Parr Noel. 84.
Peacock Charley. 86.
Peake. 21.
Peake R. 31.
Pearman Bill. 81.
Peck Dolly. 51, 52.
Petchey. 21.
Petchey W.L. (Bill). 31, 32, 64.
Petts Fred. 85.
Pidgeon Len. 71, 103.
Pinnock Bob. 26, 28, 81.
Plowright Eric. 71.
Plowright R. 11.
Plowright T. 11.
Plumley Stan. 87.
Pooley. 13.
Pooley Sid. 117.
Pottle Percy. 87.
Raspberry Eric. 71.
Raven Bob. 86, 96.
Reeve. 40.
Reeve G.W. 31, 75.
Reid D.H. (Douglas). 23, 27, 31, 32, 78, 80, 86.
Register. 21.
Reynolds Siddy. 64.
Riches B. 27.
Riches B.J. 132.
Riches Claud(e). 40, 41, 51.
Riches G. 24.
Riches R. 13.

Richman W.C. (Charles). 88, 89.
Ringer Herbert E. 6.
Ringer Horace Lock. 6.
Ringer T Allen. 31, 32.
Roberts Jack. (Bob). 88, 113.
Robertson D. 13.
Robinson John. 21.
Rockett Alice. 52, 53.
Rockett Lily. 52.
Rodwell Charley. 129.
Roome Sandra. 81.
Rose Jim. 47.
Rose Johnny. 114.
Rose William. 41.
Rout Dan. 29, 60.
Rout Ken. 64.
Rout L. 27.
Rout Reg. 48, 56, 57, 66,70, 97, 114, 119.
Royle R.J. 27.
Russell. 21.
Russell Claud. 64.
Rust. 49.
Rust F. 27.
Rust Jimmy. 43.
Ryan Mancell. 57, 74, 75, 112.
Ryan Paul. 129.
Sampson Albert. 108.
Sampson Bill. 116.
Sands Cecil. 27, 56, 59, 86, 96.
Saunders L. 27.
Savage I. 10.
Say Fred. 43.
Say Stan. 41, 57.
Scott Robert. 61.
Sedgewick Cyril. 126.
Self Jack. 108.
Senter Nevil. 128.
Shaftoe. 9.
Sharpin. 9.
Shaul D. 12.
Shaw H. 27.
Sheard Bob. 87.
Shearman. 21.
Shearman J. 27.
Shears Derek. 87, 111.
Sheppard A.C.K. 14, 29, 78, 79, 94.
Sheppardson S. 27.
Sherriff. 21.
Sibson Professor. 90.
Simpson Harry. 128.
Sizeland Joe. 126.
Skerritt J. 24.

Skerritt W. 12.
Skerry. 10.
Skipper Fred. 56, 57.
Skipper George. 85.
Smalley B. 11.
Smith. 9, 10, 70.
Smith E. 12.
Smith Fred. 43.
Smith G. 13.
Smith H. 11
Smith J. 12.
Smith Jack. 100.
Smith Leonard. 36, 40, 41, 42, 51, 59,   61, 63, 106.
Smith W.R. 106.
Snape Tom. 24, 45, 83, 84, 85, 118,   121.
Soden Tom. 70.
Softley. 10.
Spaxman. 21.
Spaxman Dave. 57.
Spinks Mrs A .(See Rockett).
Starkings P. 87, 89.
Stevens Colin. 92, 103.
Stewart Jimmy. 75.
Stinton. 21, 56.
Stinton B. 11.
Stinton L. 24.
Stinton S. 12.
Stinton Sammy. 44, 58.
Stinton T. 10.
Stinton W. 11.
Stokes C.W.K. 80.
Stokes F. (Fred). 27, 75, 96.
Suggett. 14.
Suiter. 21.
Suiter W. 27.
Targett B. 27.
Targett Bert. 85.
Targett B.M. 14, 29, 77, 79.
Taylor A. 27.
Taylor E. 27.
Taylor F. 27, 31.
Taylor Fred. 43, 44, 85.
Taylor Tom. 21, 129.
Taylor W. 14.
Thompson Ken. 87.
Thorne Percy. 77.
Thurlow Jack. 85, 86.
Thurston. 21.
Thurston W.L. 15.
Thwaite Robert. 26.
Thwaite Walter. 26, 27, 100.

Tice H. 24, 96.
Tice Percy. 96, 100.
Tinker. 9.
Tinker. (Boy). 9.
Todd Jack. 108.
Truffit C. 14.
Truffitt C.E. 90.
Turney J. 24.
Twite E. 14.
Twite Ted. 83.
Twite Walter. 100.
Vaughan W. (Bill). 27, 48, 168, 117,   129.
Voelcker Dr Augustus. 5, 90.
Wagg. 10.
Wain Bert. 84, 117.
Walden Pat. 87.
Walker 'Jock.' 127.
Ward Harold. 110.
Ward Johnny. 57.
Waterson J. 12.
Waterworth Stan. 88, 89.
Watson Bert, 108.
Watson G. 27.
Watson George. 85.
Watson W. 27.
Watson Walter. 84, 85.
Webber Don. 114.
Wellingham John. 6.
West G. 27.
West Jack. 27.
West Walter. ('Wacker'). 27, 43, 112.
Westmoreland F. (Freddy). 27, 44.
Whiley Ron. 84.
White 'Biddy.' 56.
White Tony. 75, 96, 97.
Whitely. 10.
Whittome S.A. 25.
Whiffen Charley. 71.
Wilkinson Geoff. 92.
Williamson John. 90, 92, 122, 129.
Williamson Mrs. 79.
Wilson F.T. (Fred). 61, 64, 112, 113.
Winterbone Bob. 81.
Woodhouse Ernie. 47.
Woodhouse Sid. 87.
Woodruff. 56.
Worth G.A. 31.
Wright 'Arn't'. 46.
Yarham Bert. 110.
Yates Percy. 52.